WITHOUT RIGHT & LEFT

WITHOUT RIGHT & LEFT

Nursultan Nazabaev

Translated from the Russian
by
Paula Garbp and Cynthia Carlile

CLASS PUBLISHING • LONDON

CLASS PUBLISHING
PO Box 1498
London
W6 7RS, UK

ISBN 1 872362 10 9 (H/Back)
ISBN 1 872362 11 7 (Soft)

A CIP catalogue record for this book
is available from the British Library

Printed in Great Britain

CONTENTS

vii From the Publishers

1 The Black Bread of Childhood

23 My First Teachers

37 Seniority at the Furnace

53 A Vicious Circle

69 How Problems Were Solved

83 Sons of the Times

99 The Force of Inertia

115 When Others Pay for Mistakes

129 To Be Or Not To Be

145 Epilogue

From the Publishers

Readers in the Soviet Union are tired of the many controversial political books that have appeared on the market in recent years. They are tired not because of an abundance of information, which is natural and even necessary in any civilized society, but because of the nature of this information. A tornado of accusations and exposes against prominent political leaders and whole political groups have whipped up passions not only at demonstrations, but also within families. It is truly a challenge to make sense of the labels hurled in every direction. Even those who try the hardest to understand who is a democrat, liberal, conservative, or a reactionary are at a loss to distinguish the left from the right.

People are weary of anxiety and disillusionment, of feeling so hopeless. They yearn for a tough leader (a relapse of a dangerous illness) not because they do not want to live better, but because they fear even worse times. Indeed, it will not take long before we hit the bottom. Perhaps it is time for us to take a moment to look at where we are, who we are, and whether we are not still groping in the dark, bumping only into the debris of our old world, or whether there may be some glimmer of light.

This need to stop and look around gave the publishers the idea for this somewhat unusual book. It is not an autobiography or an interview. The author simply tells us everything about himself that he felt was important. However, we reserved the right to ask questions that are so often left unanswered.

One reason we chose Nursultan Nazarbaev for this book was because the first President of Kazakhstan is so popular at home and abroad. Popularity, however, can be dangerous, especially when it becomes an end in itself, because that is when a leader can begin to think the end justifies the means. Genuine popularity is always the result of other aspirations that have nothing to do with the ego. Although we have come to know Nazarbaev better than most of our readers, we do not want to impose our own opinion of his personal qualities. We hope that this book provides plenty of food for thought and for drawing one's own conclusions. Since political events are moving at such a dynamic pace, it is relevant to know that this book was born in April 1991, in Alma-Ata, the capital of Kazakhstan.

CHAPTER ONE

The Black Bread of Childhood

Admittedly, I did not understand at first what the poet meant when he said, "He is blessed who has visited this world in its darkest days." Perhaps the literary critics will not agree with me, but I think that what Fyodor Tyutchev meant was that special insight that enables a person to embrace with gratitude not only the good in life, but also the dramatic events that bring no reward other than a keen sense of the meaning of life. Perhaps this feeling is something like that of a drifter who finally sees light at the end of the tunnel and realizes where he has come from and where he is going, and what the final goal is of his hard and lonely travels.

In some ways we are like this pilgrim. Today it seems as though we are no longer groping in the dark for solid ground under our feet. It is dangerous, however, to trip, to return to the familiar crooked paths. In such cases it has become common to recall the lessons of the past. This past we talk about and argue about so much is essentially my own life, and the life of my loved ones.

It is shameful if a Kazakh does not know seven generations of ancestors. Even today, in a modern urban family, it is not rare to find an old grandmother who can tell the small children all about their grandfather, great grandfather, great great grandfather, etc., etc. If it were not for this tradition, and other powerful sources of memory linking the Kazakhs to their past, the people could not have withstood the tremendous forces of assimilation in this century. But this is a separate subject.

It is no wonder that our memories, especially at life's most bitter moments, usher up pictures of early childhood. It is true that children perceive the world in the most natural way and are capable of noticing the smallest and yet important details. Perhaps this is why it is so easy for me to remember what Kazakhstan was like after World War II, especially in the early 1950s when I was already an adolescent. It would seem to make sense to begin my early recollections with a description of the amazing beauty of the Ala Tau range, but what I remember best was something else altogether — constant hunger pangs.

I was always awakened before sunrise. I would harness the donkey and go to a nearby town where I would be at a bread stand by the time it opened at 6:00 a.m. I would wait in a huge line where, if I was lucky, I would eventually get bread by noon. It was heavy black bread that would hold dents when you squeezed it. I would queue up two or three times in order to bring home ten loaves. Such bread could not be stored for long, so it was sliced into small pieces that were dried in the sun. Eating such bread was a big pleasure. However the excitement was really great when our cow would calve. Usually we got milk from this cow and made a special Kazakh sour drink that we mixed with corn husks. If not for this drink, we call it *airan*, we would have perished. This was how everyone lived, not only my family.

It used to be that people boasted about their "proletarian" origins. Now the trend is to find some aristocratic blood among their ancestors. Well, there was never one aristocrat in my background. I am the son, grandson and great grandson of shepherds.

All my ancestors lived at the foot of the Ala Tau range, in the village of Chemolgan, which is in the Kaskelen District, Alma-Ata Region. A Kazakh child's surname was traditionally derived from the father's name, as was the case with most peoples since time immemorial. This is still the case in some parts of Asia today. If we had not changed our customs in accordance with the rules of the Soviet passport system, my last name would not be Nazarbayev, but Abishev.

All the members of my clan were mountain people, which made us rather uncommon in Kazakhstan where most people come from the steppes. Our family rarely came down from the mountain pastures; quite frequently they spent their winters in canyons. But when Nazarbai died suddenly, the family had to return to the valley and end its nomadic lifestyle. My father Abish was just three years old. When he was eleven he was sent to work for a well-to-do Russian family. Our village at that time was already multi-ethnic. Kazakhs lived on one side of the Kaskelenka River, and settlers from central Russia, the Don, and the Ukraine lived on the other side. They got along well together; there was enough land and water for everyone.

My father was fortunate to work as a labourer for an industrious and kind Russian family, the Nikiforovs. He quickly learned Russian and how to take care of a peasant homestead, and eventually became an indispensable worker. My father knew how to make boots, plow the land, run a mill, and turn a profit when trading at the market. He was also splendid at singing Russian and Kazakh songs. When the time came he chose a bride named Alzhan. She was also fatherless, and was the best singer in the village. I inherited some of my parents' talent; I'm actually not a bad *dombra* player. Of course, those were not idyllic years; it was a rare moment when people had time to sing and dance. As my father said, they worked so hard they sweated their guts out until their callouses bled. But to work hard was honorable. The Nikiforovs had three sons, but it was Abish who was always appointed the chief. The pay was also fair. My father never felt any discrimination by the Russians. The Kazakh and Russian families might have continued to live and work peacefully if it had not been for the fateful spring of 1929. That was the first time the people of Chemolgan heard the incomprehensible word that was hard to pronounce—collectivization. The Kazakhs had no idea that they were beginning the "transition from feudalism directly into communism." However, they got the idea quickly when good homesteads fell into decline, when frightening rumours stalked along both sides of the Kaskelenka about driving out the "kulaks."

The Nikiforovs were the first whom the over-zealous collective farm organizers uprooted. My father was not persecuted. After all, he was a labourer. In fact he was invited to join the committee of poor farmers, asked to take over the mill that was confiscated from his employer. Abish was not tempted by someone else's property; he knew better than others what work it took to get it. Cartloads of people left the village after losing everything they owned. Some of them were sent to other parts of Kazakhstan, and others even farther, to the North. New settlers came to Chemolgan. They were "kulaks" from other areas, only they were not allowed to farm there. They were forced to build a road in the mountain with picks and mattocks. This serpentine road, decades later, is still referred to by the locals as the "convicts' highway".

The Kazakh steppe was beset by terrible times. Today we realize that there was no theoretical or economic basis for forced collectivization in the republic. This dramatic situation was further worsened by some of the local administrators who for their own personal benefit, aggravated hostilities and accelerated the already unrealistic rapid pace at which the population was making the transition from a nomadic life.

In his speech to the 8th Congress of the Russian Communist Party, Vladimir Lenin warned the impatient leftists not to impose on the Asian peoples the central Russian model of class struggle: "Can we approach these people and tell them that we shall overthrow their exploiters? We cannot do this . . . In such cases we have to wait until the given nation develops . . ." [V. I. Lenin, *Collected Works*, Progress Publishers, Moscow, 1980, Vol. 29, p. 172]. However, the ultra-revolutionaries were impatient. One such party functionary was F. I. Goloshchekin, who headed the Territory Communist Party Committee between 1925 and 1933. His favourite saying was "Better too much salt than too little." He was the one who thought up the misanthropic slogan that the broom of the October Revolution should sweep up the Kazakh village, which ended in great tragedy for the Kazakh people. The nomad Kazakh was robbed of his only source of food and livelihood — his livestock. The animals died without feed and care in the collective farms, and the people died of hunger. According to the 1926 census, the population of Kazakhstan was 3,628,000, but by 1939, it was barely 2,000,000. Hundreds of thousands of people died of starvation. About 1,500,000 Kazakhs left the republic, 400,000 of whom never returned.

My father took his family into the mountains and took up livestock herding and a nomadic lifestyle. These events left an impact on him for the rest of his life.

I remember when I was a young steel worker and a delegate to the Young Communist League Congress in 1962, I came home with so many stories to tell. I got so excited telling my father and our guests all about Khrushchev, about his speech to the congress, especially emphasizing his optimistic predictions about agriculture and closing the gap between town and country. I was so overwhelmed by the attention I was getting from the elders that I did not notice the mockery in their eyes. My father had been watching me with barely concealed contempt. When I started criticizing the idea of having garden plots, claiming they were blocking the way to a bright future, Abish could no longer contain himself. He lashed out at me:

"That's enough, Son. We hear too many of those speeches on the radio. You tell us this: has everyone in Moscow lost their memory? Do they want the people to starve to death again as in the thirties? A farmer without a plot is like a shepherd without any sheep. Don't take this personally, Sultan (that's what they called me at home), but this is not good news you've brought."

I made up for this mistake many years later when I finally brought back some good news from Moscow. I had met with Mikhail Gorbachev in the Kremlin where we talked about boosting the output of meat in Kazakhstan. I suggested what was really a seditious idea at that time. I said we should not limit the private plots of farmers, but do everything to encourage them. If a villager wanted to have two cows, fine, or ten, great. Gorbachev supported me, and took the risk of approving the experiment in our republic. I'd like to stress that this was long before the March 1987 Plenary Session of the CPSU Central Committee that gave the green light to the private sector. There was no talk yet of leasing or private farming.

As soon as I got back from Moscow I went to see my fellow villagers who, incidentally, had elected me their representative in the national parliament. I told them about this resolution. When I saw their happy faces I acutely missed my father who was no longer among us. The wise Abish never lived to see these days, and to hear the news that was so reassuring to the farmers.

I must admit that the results of this new approach (although there is nothing novel about private farming) surprised even me. By the end of 1987, per capita meat output in the republic increased by five kilograms, and continued to increase at an unprecedented pace. Between 1975 and 1985 output had increased by only two kilograms, but in the past five years it rose by twelve. This was possible without the government having to spend anything. We had just opened a little hole in a closed door that had held back natural initiative and entrepreneurship among the farmers. In the oppressive atmosphere of a controlling system we had simply given people a taste of freedom.

What a pleasure it is to breathe freely! This I know from my childhood. Although my father joined the collective farm (he had no choice), he stayed in the mountains and herded the collective farm's flock. Kazakhs knew that when you have sheep, livestock, you won't perish. So that's where I was born—in a mountain camp. It was 1940.

A calamity befell us: the winter camp caught on fire. My father burned himself badly trying to fight the fire—especially his arm. Despite all the efforts of the healers, his arm could no longer bend, and began to wither. That's why he was not drafted into the army a year later when the war started. But those terrible war years did not pass by our family. I know from the recollections of the elders that those years were like one long winter night marked by hunger and cold. The worst fear we had was of the wolves. Later on when I grew up I realized why my mother would turn pale whenever she heard their horrifying howls. She was not afraid of the wolves themselves because she knew that my father, even with one arm, would get rid of them. She was afraid they might kill a sheep, and then what would we say to the collective farm bosses? No excuses were accepted in those days. If you did not protect the flock you would get ten years in a forced labour camp.

Only the brief mountain summer brought some joy. The colourful summers were not only beautiful, but offered good food. Sugar, bread, and tea, all these "delicacies," were practically inaccessible. What we did have in abundance were sweet roots, juicy berries, and other treats that my mother taught me how to gather. That is how we lived. What I treasure most from my childhood was the blue skies over the snow-capped Ala Tau Mountains, bright sunshine and wonderful mountain fresh air.

I have clear recollections of the early postwar years. That was when I left the mountains for the first time with my parents to go to Chemolgan. People were celebrating Victory Day. I had never seen so many people. My mother was also seeing many things for the first time. She had never seen Balkars, Chechens, Germans, or Meskhetian Turks. Our once quiet village was filled with all sorts of people because of the terrible war. Apparently there was some relaxation of regulations after the war because some of the "kulaks" who had been exiled during the 1930s were able to return to Chemolgan. The Nikiforovs also came back, except for the father who had died so far away from home.

When I remember those days I find many things surprising. Life was completely different. Take, for example, the language issues we have in Kazakhstan today, and in many other republics. In those days, no one even thought about such problems. It was quite natural to know two languages, and even more. My father could speak the language of the deported Balkars, and was accepted by them. And how could I have lived among Russians as a six-year-old who had never heard one Russian word if the Russians had not known Kazakh? Within a year I was speaking pretty good Russian. I was also able to converse with the Balkars and Turks, and could understand the Chechens. I could even exchange a few words with the German children. Today it is hard to understand how we lost this precious gift of inter-ethnic relations, how we could have been so careless with our wealth of languages. It certainly is true that we do not treasure what we have, but regret what we lose.

In September 1990, an explosion went off in a school in Alma-Ata where the children had instruction in both Russian and Kazakh. The whole city of one million people felt the shock. Luckily no one was hurt. Despite the efforts of investigators, no suspect was ever found. Some people think that the explosion was set off by children, but I think that they had help from some adults with political aims. Evidence shows that the center of the explosion was the steel fence that divided the school building into two parts — Kazakh and Russian. The fence appeared when officials in the department of education decided the school should have two principals, and two absolutely different sets of teachers. Naturally two bears in one cave never get along. So a struggle for "sovereignty" began that ended in putting up a "border zone." It was very much like the separatist games that have become quite the fad in our parliaments. It never occurred to the teachers that they were dividing the children according to their ethnic background, and essentially installing the bomb that, by all the laws of dramatic conflict, had to go off sooner or later.

Today I wonder how many fences they would have had to put up in my small and plain Russian-Kazakh school in Chemolgan if it had not been for the wonderful teachers to whom I am so grateful, if instead we had been taught by today's champions of "ethnic purity"? We had Russian and Kazakh classes, and they were attended by children of both nationalities. There was nothing unusual about a Ukrainian or a Chechen child being taught in Kazakh. I remember attending Kazakh classes at first, and six years later switching over to Russian instruction, and again in the tenth grade going back to Kazakh.

Of course, boys will be boys. We fought over neighbourhood territory. But the fighters were never allied according to nationality. This was not even possible since a Kazakh home would be next door to a Meskhetian Turk's, and the next one might be a German's or a Russian's.

They say people tend to idealize the past as they grow older. Perhaps this is so. But to me friendship between nations was never anything abstract; it was always reflected in the simple human feeling of pleasure that comes from being with people you live with and respect. It really is a shame that we have stopped using the word friendship and instead say "inter-ethnic relations."

I realize that it is not always productive to compare the past and present. It is easy to be swayed by nostalgia, by subjectivism. However, when I look at the unhappy and sometimes angry faces of my countrymen I cannot help but wonder how this happened. Could life now be so much worse than it was before? I don't think it is. Life in the forties and fifties was harder than it is today, even taking into account the empty store shelves and rise in crime. I think this widespread pessimism is because people are tired of disillusionment, tired of living for some illusory bright future without getting anything in the present. People have lost the hope that my generation certainly possessed. Most importantly we forgot how to work, especially during the corrupting two decades of the Brezhnev era. In Asia they say that if a prophet is wrong, a whole nation trips over him. The corruption and lies of that era undermined the moral health of the nation much more than the repressive measures of the Stalin period.

Today we talk a lot about instilling good work habits in the young, but in my school days that was not even an issue. If someone had said that children have to be taught to respect work, we would have probably thought the person was crazy. After all, we don't talk about how necessary it is to breathe.

After the war, in the late forties and early fifties, my mother was given a hectare of beets to work for the collective farm. It required back-breaking labour from spring until nearly the first snowfall. Imagine, after sowing, working the whole hectare of beets by hand under the scorching sun without straightening your back. That's something a person remembers a lifetime. When the beets ripened they had to be cut with a big knife, loaded up and handed over to the collective farm. For this we would receive a certificate for one and half sacks of sugar from the Burundai sugar mill. That was all we earned. We did not get one kopek for all that work.

I remember my father was supposed to plant several hectares of wheat on a mountain slope and give the whole yield to the farm. When the wheat ripened, my father and I cut it by hand, through the night by the light of the moon. We attached a rake to the scythe so the ears would rest on one side. In two or three hours of such work we had terrible backaches. We cut the wheat while my mother made the sheaves that we later took to the centre of the collective farm where they were put into threshers.

My father worked mainly with the lifestock. It would not be exactly true if I said that my father worked day and night. I simply don't remember when he slept or when he sat down for a minute without doing some kind of work. Since my father was trained by well-to-do Russians, he knew farming very well. Although he was practically illiterate he knew how to cross fruit trees. Everyone came to his garden to see the wonders he performed on wild fruit or on the Oporto apple trees that had pears growing on one side.

Nowhere else did I see the kind of apples my father grew. He managed to preserve these apples until Spring. In March and April he would sell them at the market for a much higher price than when they were in season. A big problem was that it was 45 kilometers from Chemolgan to Alma-Ata, and it was easy to be robbed on the way since the load was driven by a horse. Another source of income was clover, which we planted after the first potato harvest. Clover was valuable as fodder and also sold well.

I am recalling all of this because it shows that we worked very hard on the collective farm but we survived due to our family plot. Only one time can I remember receiving seven lightly filled sacks of wheat in return for our labour. I think there were three or four centres in them. We carted these sacks from the centre of the collective farm. We were so happy and proud of our accomplishment.

Later we started to lose this land (half a hectare), a little at a time. We also had to finally give up the horse my father loved so much, because we were no longer allowed to keep an animal; the farm needed the fodder. One day I could not believe my eyes when I saw my father cutting down his own apple trees. It was so he would not have to pay taxes on them. We hardly had anything to eat in the house, just tea and sometimes sugar. We had to give so much butter from our cow to the farm that all we had left was skim milk.

Many things can be explained, but when you start thinking, it really does not make sense that such industrious people could end up with so little.

My only desire then was to find myself a job and help out the family. After all, I was the oldest amoung four children. We also lived with my father's niece, my mother's niece, and my grandmother. Next door lived my father's mute cousin. He was an enormous man of practically supernatural strength who was amazingly warm to everyone.

Although I was eager to continue my eduction, I still had only one thought — to hurry up and go to work to help the family. In any case, we saw that the students who came to our village were living in poverty because in those days there really weren't any stipends to speak of.

School was not hard for me. When I went to the first grade my parents did not yet have their own home. They were nomads who in summer lived in the mountains, and in the winter they camped in the steppes. That's why I lived with my paternal uncle until I was in the fourth grade. I was awakened for school early in the morning by the roosters; there were no alarm clocks. I walked, half in my sleep, through the snow for six or seven kilometers. I would arrive at five or six o'clock. If the guard was kind he would let me into the school while he got the stove going. I could get some more sleep lying next to it.

The only time to do homework was at night because the farm work had to be done first. I had to feed the livestock, clean up the shed, fetch water and work in the garden. But I learned to value time. I managed to get my homework done, and even had an hour or so for reading, which I took a liking to. Of course, my reading was not at all systematic. I read anything I could get my hands on in the school library. Luckily for me the library was not bad. I was able to read much of Pushkin, Lermontov, Leo Tolstoy, Gorky, and our Kazakh classics, such as Musrepov, Mustafin, Auezov, and Mukanov. What my friends and I liked most, however, were science fiction and adventure books. We were fascinated by the extraordinary, unfamiliar and exciting world of the heroes of Dumas, Conan Doyle, Belyaev, Haggard and Cooper. We tried to bring this world alive in our games. We had our own Chemolgan Musketeers and Sherlock Holmeses, red-skinned Indians and white-faced trackers. In those days life in cities and in the countryside was very different. Whatever was accessible and realistic for boys in the city was often no more than a dream for us. We were much closer to the prose of everyday existence, and the concerns of just putting some food on the table. This is why we had such modest demands on our future and had to be more realistic in evaluating our own potential.

I do not know exactly why I decided to become a geologist. Perhaps I was influenced by the newspapers. When I was in my last years of school I read many articles and heard many radio programmes about the construction of Kazakhstan's steel plant, about how young people were needed to run it. For some reason I associated geology with mining operations. My father did not know what a geologist was, but one winter something unexpected happened to him. When he was driving his herd from the mountain into the steppes, he came upon a geological expedition. The geologists were lost and were on the verge of dying. They were lying in the sand, helpless from lack of strength. Their horses had died and the camel had wandered off. My father fed them and took them to his camp. When he came home he had only one question for me: "Is that the kind of geologist you want to be?"

However, my father realized that I had to get an education. Although my mother and father could barely read themselves, they had high regard for people who were literate. Incidentally, Kazakhs have always respected knowledgeable people. It also helped that the school principal and teachers visited our home and all of them said I had to continue my education. My father also saw that young people who were my seniors were not able to help their families no matter how hard they worked. It is no wonder that when I finished the seven-year education, the whole family was unanimous in sending me on. That is when I left my village for the first time. It was not far away, to the district centre called Kaskelen, where there was a ten-year boarding school.

I realized then that my parents were making a big sacrifice by giving up a potential worker and breadwinner. Therefore, when I came home on weekends and holidays, I worked as hard as I could to help with the chores. And, as before, the summer vacation was no time for rest either. Right after the school year ended I would either work in the fields by home or in the mountains.

I graduated from school during Khrushchev's promotion of the chemical industry. Lenin had said that communism was Soviet power plus electrification of the country. Since Soviet power and electrification were plentiful, and communism had not materialized yet, Khrushchev decided to add chemicalization to the formula.

In short, I decided to major in chemistry at Kazakh State University. This time my father supported me at once. He had apparently also heard all the talk on radio about the importance of the chemical industry. He also liked reading the newspapers, although he could not write. Our family was the first in our village to buy a radio. I think that was in 1954, during one of our trips to the market at Alma-Ata. As I now remember, the box was called Moskvich. At first the whole block would come to listen to this strange "live voice" we had in our home.

Perhaps I should not bother telling the story of my unsuccessful attempt to enter the university. But it left an impact on me for years to come. After all, there was no one in our clan, not even a distant relative, who had a higher education. I can't forget how my father sold the only bull from our only cow, and gave all the money to me. I realized full well what this meant for the family, and so I decided not to use the money unless it was absolutely necessary. My father told me just before I left for Alma-Ata that people bribed their way into university. There were six people in my dormitory room who were taking the entrance exams. Three of them, including myself, were common folk, and the other three were the children of officials. One of their fathers was secretary of, I think, the Urals regional party committee, another father was secretary of one district party committee of the Alma Ata Region, and the third one was also a leading official, although I do not remember what his position was. We village boys studied day and night for the exams, but our room-mates partied around the clock, since they had plenty of money. They went to the park and to dances. It was clear from the outset that at least two of them did not know anything.

Naturally all three of the "partying" boys passed their exams. During my oral exam in chemistry, the most important one I had to take, the professor kept me answering questions for an hour and a half. But I still got a five, the highest grade. The bias against me, however, affected the grades of my other exams. As a result I did not have a high enough score to enter. The professor who had quizzed me on chemistry for an hour and a half, and therefore knew how good I was at the subject, made an appeal to the admissions commission, but that did not help.

Amazingly, I was not nearly as indignant about this then as I am now. Apparently we were brought up to be submissive. My father would always tell me not to be pushy, to leave things well enough alone, and not to criticize anyone in leadership. I am only now beginning to understand that he was conditioned this way himself — to accept things as they were just to keep from being convicted, to keep from being arrested. I can understand him. He lived through the purges of the thirties. And he learned a lot from the hard labor he did on the Turkmenian-Siberian Railway construction. Incidentally, he was an outstanding worker, and in 1936 he received a certificate signed by Stalin for setting a work record.

After I failed to get into the university, my life returned to normal, but not for long. As I already said, one of the main sources of our modest income was what we earned from the clover we grew. We dried and tied the clover and got it ready to take to market. I could not wait for my father to name the day. The night before we loaded the cart, and at four in the morning we set off for Alma-Ata. By ten o'clock we were at the market. Naturally I did not stay put at the market. My father gave me a whole ruble from the money we would make from the sales, and I went off to walk in that wondrous city and to go to the movies.

As I walked down the street I noticed some people in blue uniforms—three pilots who were leaving the market with full bags of cucumbers. Suddenly a crazy childhood dream came back to me — to become a pilot. What boy in those days did not have that dream, I followed them for a long time, but did not have the courage to talk to them. Finally I tapped one of them on the arm.

"Excuse me, can I talk to you?" I asked.

I looked so nervous and so desperate that the pilots were stunned at first. I mixed Kazakh and Russian words together, something I never did before, in my efforts to find out how to apply for flying school. I wanted to know where I could find such a school, and what I had to do to get in. To prove my worth I even pulled out my diploma. I had it with me at all times just in case I could show it to someone who would see that I had all A's, and only one B.

The pilots finally understood what I wanted from them and moved over to the side of the street to discuss it. The eldest of them took off his cap, scratched his head, and smiled as he looked at my diploma. He winked at his friend and said, "A straight-A student. He could get into a university, let alone a flying school."

I picked up one of the bags and went with them down the street where the republic's civil aviation department was located. On the way I found out that the pilots were from Kiev and in a few hours they had to go home. I was really lucky, because that day the aviation department had begun taking applications for the Kiev Institute of Aviation.

From then on events developed at whirlwind speed. I wrote my application with the help of my new friends. One of the officials looked at my diploma, wrote down the information about my identification papers that I told him, and gave me a medical form to be filled out by a health clinic. He said I could bring the rest of my documents later. I went to the health clinic with that form, and by the end of the day I knew I was fit. All that was left was to pass the entrance exams.

I rushed back to the market. I was floating on cloud nine. But the closer I got the slower and less confident was my pace. When I saw my father was annoyed because I was late, I decided not to say anything. I did not say anything later when I had to go to Alma-Ata to take the exams, and simply made up a story. Only a month later, when I saw with my own eyes that I was accepted, I got the courage to tell my family.

I don't even like to remember what happened next. My mother was in tears over the thought of me going so far away to Kiev, and to fly at that! "Your parents didn't bring you into the world for you to end up killing yourself," she wailed. My father did not say much. He just told me to be sure to be home that night. That evening all our relatives came, and all the elders of Chemolgan. Abish invited them all; he didn't forget anyone. The council began its deliberations.

I won't repeat the bitter words I had to hear that night from my fellow villagers. What they said in essence was that I had no right to uproot myself from the land that had given me food and water, and to carry on with my life in secrecy, away from others. I was very upset, but perhaps that was the first time I felt such a strong bond with my fellow villagers. I realized that my life and my troubles mattered to them. In short, the next day, despite my agony, I withdrew my application.

Perhaps the young readers will think I was weak. It's true that today's youth make their own decisions, and that's fine. But I sincerely think that young people do not always show enough sense of responsibility for their actions to warrant their independence. Sometimes egoism takes the upper hand when they have to make a moral choice, or a moral evaluation.

Of course, I could have insisted on doing what I wanted. No one had forbidden me to go. But respect for elders was the cornerstone of our upbringing; it was absolutely unthinkable to begin any undertaking without the blessings of our parents. I do not think that was the worst quality of my generation. We got this conditioning from childhood. My father taught me that when you see an elder, whether you know him or not, you must say hello first. I remember how the adults would light up when you'd say to them, "Assalau Maleikum." The answer was always, "Whose son are you?" According to another custom, when you were coming home after a long absence you had to stop by the home of the eldest person in the village to say hello and to get his blessings. Maybe that does not seem so important today, but these customs were honoured by everyone, and fathers took pride in children who followed their advice.

At that time a new city called Temirtau was the focus of attention in Kazakhstan, where one of the country's biggest steel plants was under construction. I read a newspaper ad for a Temirtau technical school that was accepting Young Communist League members to be trained for the steel plant. The course was for one year and all expenses were paid by the government.

I showed the ad to my father. When he read it he thought about it for a while, then he sighed and said, "Well, Son, go ahead and see the world. If you have troubles, come back; this is your home."

It took just two days to get a certificate from our Young Communist League office. The goodbyes were short, I got in a train and set off for Temirtau. Talking to some passengers I learned that the work would be hard, but the pay was good. I wasn't afraid of hard work. I was reassured of my decision by the expectation that I could help support my family.

In the beginning of your story you mentioned how most people felt an inner liberation in the past few years. After all, our eyes have been opened to the absurdities of many aspects of our life, to things that used to seem quite normal. Wasn't this enlightenment too long in coming? Or perhaps we understood all this earlier but we were better off ignoring these feelings and going with the flow?

Under the totalitarian administrative-command system, not only the economy was stagnant, but every sphere of life, the ideology and relations between people. Social apathy was rampant, and became worse under the Brezhnev cult, especially in the late seventies and early eighties. This cult was shaped mainly in Moscow by Brezhnev's team, by the Politburo and Central Committee Secretaries. This disease spread throughout the whole party and government structure, from top to bottom, and in all the republics. Brezhnev selected the party Central Committee leaders in the republics, and they in turn appointed the heads of regional committees completely on the basis of personal loyalty. The powerful filter provided by the apparatus allowed for no mistakes. For instance, to become first secretary of the regional committee a candidate had first to be interviewed in the republic's Central Committee, and then in the CPSU Central Committee at all the hierarchic levels. At the highest level the person had to be interviewed by two or three members of the Politburo, then by the second in command, and then by the General Secretary of the whole party. After that his candidacy was discussed at the Secretariate and Politburo meetings. This was not a democratic process by any means. A recommendation from the national Central Committee made the appointment final. The plenary session of the regional party committee was held only to rubber-stamp this decision.

Sometimes this procedure was criticized locally, especially when someone was appointed from the outside and was completely unknown. However the concept of party discipline required total submission to the higher bodies. Whole areas of the country were beyond reproach because they were headed by close friends of the General Secretary. This was true of Kazakhstan, Uzbekistan, the Ukraine, and a number of other regions.

When Yuri Andropov took over attempts were made to bring order to economic and social spheres. Ordinary people gave their approval. But nothing fundamental could be accomplished without changing the whole system of relations within the apparatus, and in society as a whole. That is why the decisions passed at the April 1985 plenary session of the CPSU Central Committee were supported by the people. There was an explosion of enthusiasm in 1985 and 1986. People began working better, and it looked like things would improve. I think the people trusted the new party leadership and believed it was capable of improving the situation.

Did all the party leadership in that previous era conform to the circumstances at all times?

I personally cannot say yes to that question, because I know that there were honest people among the leadership. We have to look at the nature of the circumstances. Undoubtedly we all felt humiliated to see that our great country was governed by old and ailing people unable to say anything coherent without reading from their notes. But it was necessary to compromise with the situation, otherwise the well-oiled system would toss out anyone. The mechanism of party penalties worked perfectly, and we all know what it meant to be expelled from the party.

Of course, many people preferred to close their eyes to all this in order to enjoy life's comforts. But such types have always existed in every society. It is also true that decent people were misled. They accepted the stereotypes that had developed over the decades. I would like to discuss this more later on.

You have mentioned ethnic relations a few times and noted that issues that used to seem so simple and clear are now so complex—with tragic consequences. You talk about the friendly relations between different ethnic groups in the republic. Yet you also say that the Kazakh people were the victims of forced assimilation in this century. Aren't you contradicting yourself?

I do not think you should confuse these two concepts—friendly ethnic relations in our great common nation, and forced assimilation, which, as we know, was the lot not only of Kazakhs in this country. To me there is a clear line between such phenomena as the great nation ambitions of the former "leaders" and sincere friendly feelings toward people of any other nationality. The latter attitude is basic to the ordinary Russian people who have worked the land all their lives or who have stood next to me at the steel furnaces and helped me find my way in life. I would disagree completely with anyone who claims that there was never understanding between the peoples of the USSR. This is either a deliberate lie or reflects basic poor knowledge about life and history. I think that every mature person can cite many examples of his/her own personal experience. I witnessed the best of relations between different nationalities in the Kazakhstan steel plant, the Turkmenian-Siberian Railway, the Bolshoi Balkhash, and Dzhezkazgan. There were also always good relations between the various republics. Of course, some of the native ethnic groups felt discriminated against to some extent. It's no wonder they developed a desire to be on their own. But, first, this never had a serious impact on interpersonal relations, and, second, it's simply criminal to blame all these problems on the Russian people, or any other.

Historically Kazakhstan has developed an ethnically diverse population. We are also neighbours to the peoples of Central Asia, Eastern Siberia, and the multi-ethnic Sinkiang-Uigur autonomous region of China. The Russian people have played a special role in Kazakhstan's history. I believe that Kazakhs, and people of all other nationalities have always intuitively realized that it is their destiny to live together, to live in harmony and friendship. Without this feeling it would be impossible for them to conduct their lives. This feeling has been passed on from generation to generation, from parents to children, from children to grandchildren. In my opinion this enabled the peoples of our entire region to avoid negative attitudes toward one another that were sometimes deliberately generated. This issue deserves thorough and objective analysis. Social scientists have a great deal to study. If we want to weed out these bad attitudes that come to the fore from time to time, we have to understand the origins of their roots and seeds.

We are still trying to deal with ethnic conflicts without really understanding their history. No wonder — especially in view of the fact that since the 1917 socialist revolution everything was done to make the Kazakh people forget their own history. Even in pre-revolutionary Kazakhstan, where illiteracy prevailed, there were always two or three people who could read and write. Written history and a wealth of literature developed over the centuries. What explanation is there for the fact that in the 1930s the Arabic alphabet was replaced first with the Roman alphabet and then, with the Cyrillic? I think this was done deliberately, since the Marxists argued that it was necessary to eliminate the differences between ethnic groups. So they began to wipe out the memory of the people, and the best qualities were forgotten first because the bad are more resilient. Whether we like it or not it is no accident that the Kazakh people feel that they were hurt. It could not have been otherwise when the languages, cultures, and traditions of native peoples were stifled in the region.

I think that if we revive the history, shed light on the past, we can remove the causes of this misunderstanding between peoples which sometimes develops. I am simply amazed how official Soviet historians managed to turn everything upside down, and not just contemporary history. For instance, the struggle between Kenesara Kasymov's forces and the tsarist colonizers that was waged in the 1830s and 1840s is presented as a purely nationalistic, feudal movement against the interests of the people.

At the same time nothing is said about the forced colonization of Kazakhstan which was especially intense in the 19th century. In the more recent period there was the campaign for collectivization which was intended to inculcate the idea of proletarian revolution among nomadic and steppeland Kazakhs. This is presented as a great service to the people. The result, however, was quite different: the only means of existence was taken away from the people, their livestock, which led to hundreds of thousands of deaths. Meanwhile the Stalinist purges did away with the Kazakh intelligentsia, the hope of the nation.

After World War II, Kazakhstan had the hard task of providing homes for peoples who had been deported from their homelands—the Balkars, Chechens, Ingush, Meskhetian Turks, and Crimean Tatars. It is not difficult to imagine the frame of mind these people were in when they came, having lost their homes and their native land. No one asked the local population when the decision was made to develop our virgin lands. Undoubtedly this was an economically wise decision. But hardly any of the Soviet people knew that this land was not abandoned. Kazakh herders lived there, knew how to take care of the land, preserved it, and constantly changed their pasture areas to prevent depletion. According to century-old traditions the land was divided up between the herders. There was another negative result of the development of these virgin lands: the entire country lost an important source of livestock. The area was inhabited by around two and a half million people from the European part of the Soviet Union who came to farm these lands. New large schools were built and local schools that taught in the Kazakh language were closed. The Kazakh people themselves began to think it was not necessary for their children to get instruction in their native language because all institutions of higher education and vocational schools taught exclusively in Russian. The parents of my generation were already telling us that if we wanted to become something, we would have to learn Russian. Russian was the preferred language of communication even in areas where the Kazakh population was 90–95 percent. The local intelligentsia, especially writers, poets and playwrights were losing ground. It hardly made sense to publish literature in Kazakh, because the readership was declining rapidly. Anyone who spoke out in defense of the people and the culture was accused of nationalism, such as the great Mukhtar Auezov or the prominent Soviet scientist, Kanysh Satpayev.

I recall a speech by Leonid Brezhnev in which he said that our peoples shone like the edges of diamonds, each with its own colour, its own language, and its own culture. These words were repeated over and over in the speeches of local leaders. We heard many such eloquent speeches that had nothing to do with the reality. In fact the Kazakhs were deliberately turned into second class citizens, and naturally this made them resentful. But I would like to stress once again that this resentment was not directed against ordinary Russians or other peoples. Working people lived and worked in harmony. Furthermore, because of the Russian working class Kazakhstan gained a large number of skilled Kazakh workers. Russia helped train the local engineers. Through the Russian language the Kazakhs gained access not only to the riches of the great Russian culture, but also to the outstanding accomplishments of world civilization.

We understand clearly who was responsible for all our troubles, who needed the inhuman regime, the administrative-command system. Any honest person realizes that the Russian people and Russian culture also suffered great losses under the totalitarian system. That is why we have always advocated internationalism, the consolidation of people of all nationalities, and the decisive restructuring and reform of the Union in which all peoples should develop freely. I would not, however, go into this subject in detail since it is outside the scope of this question and requires special consideration.

The bitter experience of the Kazakh people shows the consequences of forcing nomadic peoples to settle, as well as accelerating the solution of many other social issues. Intervening in the social process to speed up development usually has tragic results. Do you think that when we continually stress the "revolutionary nature" of our current reforms we are not heeding the lessons of history?

It is true that history can teach us a lot, but we do not always want to learn the lessons to avoid repeating the same mistakes. In 1985, we were told that it would take two to three years to restructure the economy. Having correctly determined what general economic reforms should be made, the leadership of the party and state, as it later turned out, had not thought seriously about reforming the political system. Declaring democratization and glasnost was not enough. No one apparently suspected that such a terrible monster would develop out of these twins without radical reforms.

I think that at first most people felt that everything would change drastically for the better by eliminating a few phenomena that irritated the people and by allowing them to express different opinions. The things that we began to fight sincerely (such as excess authority, unnecessary privileges, the stifling of criticism, bribery, and corruption) turned out to be just the tip of the iceberg, just the symptoms of the disease rather than the root cause. That is why the country is in a deep economic and political crisis. We are seeing a repeat of what happened to the reforms of the 1950s and 1960s, only the consequences now are much more severe because crude mistakes were made in the strategy.

It was unrealistic, of course, to think that in a short period it was possible to turn our whole economic and political machine in the right direction and achieve tangible results. If we look at our history over the past seven decades, we can see so many examples of a utopian approach to the solution of the most complex political, social and economic problems. It turned out later that we did not have a well thought out plan for restructuring. We began by saying that we were learning as we went along, that life itself was constantly teaching us this and that. Obviously we can't learn as we go along, but in calmer circumstances, we could have, perhaps, avoided the unwarranted experiments that I plan to talk about more in detail later. Now I would just like to point out, for instance, how we eased up on discipline and order at the work place by supposedly democratizing production, and how we hurt the cooperative sector and upset monetary circulation with a bad tax system. Each year of perestroika the number of mistakes increased in geometrical progression. A record-setting year was 1990. Now we have to reap the sad results of our latest poorly planned measures. I am not an advocate of big leaps and forced actions. Now it is clear to everyone that the transition of our society to a qualitatively new state will take a long time. But we have to make concrete advances, chart clear directions and goals that the people will trust.

According to your recollections it was possible to make changes for the better, for instance, in agriculture, even in the stifling circumstances of a totally administrative-command system. Does this mean that it is right to demand a return to 1985, as many people are saying? Isn't there some truth to this?

Of course I can understand people who make this call. Living standards have declined considerably, output has dropped, the store shelves have emptied, and social problems have been aggravated to the limit. But there is no way back. We have to understand that for too long we squandered our national wealth. We had to pay for this sooner or later. The time has come. Perestroika is not to blame. The current situation in the country is the result not only of poor policies. The old methods of economic management have already failed, and any attempt to revive them will only deepen the crisis and worsen the consequences.

Since we have already touched on the problem of agriculture, I would like to explain the situation in this area. Yes, in the last five-year-plan period we really did increase the yields of virtually everything produced in agriculture. This was accomplished mainly by lifting all restrictions in the private sector. However no radical reorganization of agriculture has taken place. We still have the old management system under which the district government controls all the farms in the area, and the directors of state farms are hanging on to their privileges, and usually put up strong resistance to any innovation, especially the introduction of leasing and private farming. At the same time around one-third of the republic's agricultural enterprises continue to operate at a loss. But this does not genuinely concern anyone in local government, because the state is still giving subsidies. The worse a state farm or a collective farm operates, the more subsidies it receives, and the wages of the employees are even higher than they are on profitable farms. And on the contrary, the better a farm works, the higher the quotas it has to reach, and the larger the percentage of the profit that is deducted and distributed among those lagging behind. Surely we cannot seriously think that under such a paradoxical system we can achieve anything substantial?

One more important circumstance has to be taken into account. The mentality of the people changes, and it is changing irreversibly. People are increasingly interested in leasing farms, setting up their own private farms. Such farms are far more efficient. Such farms are especially successful if they are raising livestock or cultivating irrigated crops. At the moment, due to Kazakhstan's specific conditions, we think it is premature to sell land to private owners. No one would be able to buy such huge territories of land that can range from 600 to 1,000 hectares. The population will not approve of this either. However I think that soon we should be able to partially privatize farming land. At any rate, we have to move forward. We have no other choice.

You have mentioned several times the difficulties in Kazakhstan in the twenties and thirties caused by assimilation, collectivization, and the Stalinist purges. More terrible trials were still ahead. The Kazakh people demonstrated exceptional courage and heroism during World War II, as is illustrated by many examples. It is enough to recall the heroism of the Panfilov Division or that of Manshuk Mametova or Alia Moldagulova. In your opinion, what were the Kazakhs fighting for?

They were fighting for the same thing as most Soviet people — for their homeland. I already stressed the thought that the Kazakhs never linked the oppression of the administrative-command system with the interests of the Russian people, or the ordinary people of any other nationality. After all, everyone suffered equally from the lawlessness of the thirties. The fate of the Nikiforovs is just one example. Furthermore, these shared calamities united different peoples even more so, and compelled them to hold on more tightly to one another. Awareness of the mortal danger hanging over the entire country also united people. I am certain that in World War II, friendship between the Soviet peoples was tested for its strength. However the source of this friendship cannot be sought in the "wise nationalities policy" as official propaganda has wanted us to believe. In fact this friendship strengthened despite the undemocratic policies of the Stalinist regime.

This year marks the fiftieth anniversary of the beginning of the sacred war of the Soviet people against the fascist occupiers. We know very well the high price that was paid for victory. Most people of my generation who did not fight in the war, including myself, have been concerned in recent years that we were unable to ensure the victorious veterans a normal life. We must always realize the debt we have to these people who, at the twilight of their life, have been stripped of much of their faith in the ideals of justice. We often hear them saying, "What did we make such sacrifices for?" I take that as a criticism of us all. At the same time we cannot let people, especially young people, question whether we needed this victory. I am personally convinced of the significance of this victory, because the most terrible evil in the history of civilization was crushed in that war. That is why one of my first steps as president of Kazakhstan was to issue a special decree on additional benefits to World War II veterans. This met with widespread approval among all the people of Kazakhstan.

CHAPTER TWO

My First Teachers

The Kazakhs have a saying equivalent to "God helps those who help themselves". I don't want to give the impression that the people I grew up among were not superstitious. However I don't remember them, even during the hardest times, throwing up their hands and letting fate take care of things. Comparisons between the past and present are inevitable when you see how bewilderment and passiveness, especially among the youth, are pervasive in our society. It is amazing that even well educated people want to believe in some fatal inevitability. Why should people strain themselves with their cares at work or at home if they can watch a national TV programme that tells them regularly what joys and successes, or, on the contrary, what difficulties and disillusionment await them the following week? All they have to do is know what star they were born under. Although I have heard some amazing predictions and coincidences, I have always been skeptical about mystics and astrologers. If I have come into contact with any "clairvoyance," it was of a totally different kind.

When I studied metallurgy in Dneprodzerzhinsk, our teachers were experienced workers. Dmitri Pogorelov was one of them. He was a man with tremendous knowledge of both the steel industry and life. He often gave us advice for everyday living, the kind that no one writes about or even talks about. For instance, he instructed us in how to get acquainted with young women and how to be selective. What he told us was much more profound and useful than the fashionable advice of psychologists and sexologists today. All of us thought of Dimitri Pogorelov as an older friend and so we confided in him. He knew us backwards and forwards. He saw right through us and knew the capabilities of each of us. Sometimes he would listen to us talking, look at us carefully and suddenly say: "Young man, you're going to be an engineer, a shop foreman, you might go to prison, and you (he was looking at me) will be the prime minister." When these friends and I meet we never cease to be amazed at how right his predictions were.

To allay any suspicions I'd like to say that I never have been excessively proud. I never had any supernatural ambitions. Life has always dictated its own laws, sometimes prosaic, and sometimes harsh. The primary problem I have always had is to endure, and hold on.

. . . Although I had my father's blessings to go to Temirtau, my parents were not the least bit enthusiastic. Karaganda and the area around it, including Temirtau, had a bad reputation at that time. My fellow villagers thought of it as a place for camps, exiles, and a conglomeration of criminals from all over the country. And the labour armies that were organized and sent there during World War II were not ideal breeding grounds of human relations. There was also a criminal group that instilled terror among the local residents. My first impression of Temirtau was that it was a tiny town in the middle of an enormous construction site. It consisted of cranes, trenches, foundation pits, heaps of metal, sand, mounds of construction waste, tents, and no roads. The first blast furnace and electric power plant were being built then. For three days we had to stay in some basement, then we moved to a dormitory across the Nura river, in the town of Tokarevka. No sooner had we started to work than all of us with a secondary education were offered a chance to go to school in Dneprodzerzhinsk. It turned out that the republic's leadership, concerned about training local people for the future plant, was in a hurry to train Kazakhs in the country's big steel centres. A total of 400 of us were sent to school. Some went to the Urals, and my group of 100 went to the Ukraine. After that it's not hard to believe in fate. It seems as though I was destined to end up on the banks of the Dnieper.

We went to Dneprodzerzhinsk via Moscow. We were simply dumbfounded to find ourselves in the capital with our bags and suitcases. The worst torture was when we went for a ride on the subway. Someone fell on the escalator, someone's heel was torn off when leaving it, someone's bag was caught in the door and waved in the wind until the next stop.

The Dneprodzerzhinsk steel plant made a bad impression of many of the newcomers including myself. The problem was that few of us had been raised in a city, although we did have some general idea about the working and living conditions of industrial workers. It's understandable how a young man from the steppes would react when seeing a steel plant for the first time in his life. The noise is thunderous, the sparks fly, and it seems that all sorts of things are whizzing through the air and falling on you. The melted cast iron runs like water in a canal, and its terrifying to go near it. The very thought that you could spend your whole life in this hell was enough to put you out of sorts. It did not help matters when one of the young men in our group passed out. So our first trip around the plant was ended abruptly. A few days later someone asked to go home. You can imagine what the workers were saying about us after all that.

However, we never heard anyone speak offensively to us. After our training I learned that a special meeting of the workers had been called to warn them that no jokes about us would be tolerated in the least. But you cannot stop people talking to each other, so rumours about the inferiority of the Kazakh boys circulated back to us. Our pride was hurt which motivated us to work even harder. Soon we got the opportunity to boost our image in the eyes of our Ukrainian counterparts.

In those days wrestling was an especially popular sport in Dneprodzerzhinsk. Strong young workers gladly belonged to wrestling teams, and worked out even after a hard shift. Once we went to the gym just to watch. When we saw these guys rolling around on the mats, we realized at once that this was our native sport, which we call kazakhsha-kures, and which is familiar to every boy in every village. These athletes did not have the belts that are customary for us, but this did not stop us. When a blond, well-built young man offered to test my strength, I agreed at once. I did not look like an athlete at all in my T-shirt and underwear. Everyone in the gym burst out laughing. I didn't care. I started off with the move my father had taught me. The laughter stopped, and my fellow Kazakhs began cheering me on. My opponent, angered by his first setback, became frantic. Then I really caught him by surprise and pinned him down to the mat by both his elbows. All he could do was shake his head, as if to say: Not bad at all Kazakhstan. He and I later became good friends. He was a wonderful Ukrainian fellow by the name of Mikola Litoshko. He even went with us to the Kazakhstan Steel Plant. We worked together in Temirtau where we produced the first Kazakh cast iron. After serving in the army he went back to the Ukraine, but we still remember each other and correspond. How could we forget each other when I was like a second son to Mikola's parents? I must admit that I almost married his sister Natasha. I don't even remember what stopped us. The Litoshko family lived in their own house on the outskirts of Dneprodzerzhinsk, and I went there practically every evening, and every Sunday. Sometimes I took along my Kazakh friends. My friend's mother was a master at pies. I'll never forget her baking; I don't think I ever ate anything more tasty. Those pies were real lifesavers when we went home for vacation. The train to Alma-Ata took a week, and food was hard to come by along the way. So we packed the pies baked by considerate Maria Ilinichna, and always had enough to eat.

After that memorable evening in the gymnasium, the workers thought much better of the future steel workers from Kazakhstan. Not only myself, but many other Kazakhs were good at wrestling, and even organized their own team that competed well at factory and city meets. We made friends, and shared common interests. We were no longer shy and isolated from the others. We got used to the work, too, and stopped jumping at every spark that flew, at every mechanism that rumbled. Fire and metal gradually became familiar and ordinary to us.

In the satire section of one of the newspapers, I once read this funny story. A shop foreman meets a group of young new engineers and accompanies them to their first meeting. He says to them: "Here you have to first forget everything you learned at college, and in a few months I'll make real engineers out of you." Yes, no college can give you what I learned in a year and a half at the Dneprodzerzhinsk vocational school. At any rate, when I later studied metallurgical sciences at college, I already knew everything, especially because I had so much practical training on site at the factory.

Of course, I owe a lot to the steel workers who taught us how to work on our own, people like Dmitri Pogorelov. Unfortunately, later we managed to turn the institution of genuine mentoring into something done simply for the sake of appearance, as was the case with so many other things.

I often hear people saying that they were either fortunate or unfortunate in meeting good people. As I look back on my first independent steps in life, and later the experience I had as a mature adult, I realize that you cannot sort people into "good" and "bad." Sometimes you know a person a year and think that you have been through everything together, but later you find out there was really no substance to the relationship. And many times the opposite happens, when you find out that a person with a difficult and unsociable personality is there for you during the worst crisis.

We live among people who are usually not of our own choosing. We don't really pick our own friends; we stumble across them as we go through life. Recently a close friend of mine for many years, Agabek Ryspanov, came to see us. He used to be a steel worker, and is now retired in Temirtau. In Dneprodzerzhinsk he was the first leader of our group. Naturally we had a little drink and began reminiscing. Suddenly he began this monologue:

"You know, Nursultan, I really hated you when you were elected the leader of the group instead of me. You have no idea how many times I wanted to kill you. I wanted to throw you off the train when we went home for vacation, but you didn't go out on the platform. Many times at the plant I wanted to push you into the casting ladle with the metal."

I must admit it was unpleasant to imagine myself lying in a ladle nothing left of me but a cloud of steam. My wife was shocked to hear this nonchalant male conversation.

This was the situation. Among the young men who went to Dneprodzerzhinsk there were some ex-convicts who had served time mainly for theft or hooliganism. One of them, Ryspanov, was a former thief and extremely strong. People were instinctively afraid of him. After all, he had even set on fire the orphanage he lived in. He was the only one of us who dressed well. He told us himself that he got the suits and fashionable shirts from an engineer he rode with on the train. Ryspanov drank with the man who was returning from the North and stole two of his suitcases. He had people shine his shoes and iron his slacks, and he was even served his food at the cafeteria.

Gradually we realized that I was just as strong as he was. Besides, I knew Russian fluently and got straight A's. That's why the others started congregating around me, and finally they elected me officially as their leader. As I found out many years later, Ryspanov was offended so much he wanted to kill me. I suppose he had enough healthy ambition to do the right thing ultimately. I remember that he began to do well in school. We were all surprised when, despite his poor Russian, he memorized entire pages from our textbooks including rules and formulas even though he wasn't able to understand the information. A few years later we found him a wife. He moved to Temirtau after he finished the Dnepropetrovsk Institute of Technology, and worked as a shift supervisor. His knowledge of technology was unsurpassed, and his colleages and subordinates were amazed by his diligence.

Every report we heard in Dneprodzerzhinsk about the construction of the Kazakhstan Steel Plant either gave cause for joy or anxiety. Would we finish in time to start up the plant? Would be be capable of running such a huge enterprise? We felt great responsibility. I recently looked over some old newspaper files and recalled the tense and at the same time festive atmosphere of those days. Many articles were written about Temirtau and reflected the general excitement. Journalists did not spare superlatives in describing the heroic builders of the country's new and huge steel plant. Everywhere it was stressed that the project was organized by the Young Communist League. Just reading those articles made us feel so enthusiastic and proud we were involved in this major national effort.

Suddenly in early August of 1959 rumours began circulating around the factory that there was trouble in Temirtau. We heard that troops were sent to the city, there were casualties, and the construction had been stopped. This news was shocking. At first we did not believe it, especially since there was nothing about it in the newspapers. The fact that the newspapers had nothing to say about the plant seemed to confirm the rumours which became more detailed by the day. I remember one of the workers in our shop, who was the rare owner of a radio, came to work with a big secret. He had accidentally tuned in to the Voice of America when Khrushchev was visiting the United States and meeting with President Eisenhower. Apparently they had the following conversation:

"What is this new city in Kazakhstan we've heard about?" asked the president.

"Temirtau," replied Khrushchev. "We're building a giant steel plant there."

"Why are the people rebelling?" inquired the president.

"There is no rebellion in Kazakhstan," protested our leader. We figured that since the events were mentioned at such a high level, there must be something to the rumours. Where there's smoke there's fire.

We finally learned the truth about the tragedy only after we finished our studies and returned home.

I graduated a skilled worker at the eighth level, two levels lower than the highest, the tenth. It was a warm April evening when I took my last stroll along a street with the statue of Prometheus that stood in a high pedestal next to the Eternal Flame. I don't know if Prometheus is still there, but they say that there is a statue of Brezhnev on that same street. Incidentally, next to our vocational school there were some small two-storey houses where they say Brezhnev's mother had lived. He had lived there himself earlier when he went to the evening classes of the metallurgical institute. People talked about this a lot in Dneprodzerzhinsk; after all, at that time Brezhnev already held high leadership positions in the government and the party.

Finally we were back in Temirtau. What surprised us most of all was the abundance of food and consumer goods in the city's stores. Dneprodzerzhinsk could not compare in this respect, so our eyes were popping. Now it is hard to believe, but the stores had plenty of black and red caviar, sturgeon, concentrated sweet milk, prize-winning cognac and wine. Clothing was available to suit any taste, including imported items. There were even expensive fur hats, but very few people actually bought them since they were 400 roubles, which was a lot of money in those days.

All this abundance was the result of Brezhnev's visit to put things in order. People say he came there right after the troubles began. He walked through the construction site, but he did not talk to any of the workers. He was accompanied by a large group of local leaders who realized that they would have to pay for what happened in Temirtau. Sure enough, many party and construction bosses were soon dismissed, and some of them were even expelled from the party. It is quite possible that these people would not have lost their jobs if it had not been for a meeting of the plant's construction workers that Brezhnev addressed. He began accusing the workers of sabotage, of political illiteracy, of having blindly followed anti-Soviet elements who were aiding world imperialism. He was especially adamant that they had disappointed Khrushchev after he had given so much fatherly help to the construction effort. This set off the crowd. The workers did not care about the difference in rank, and began showing their grievances: "If he's helping so much then why don't the workers have any meat? Why isn't housing being built? Why are the bosses robbing the stocks?"

There were so many hard questions that Brezhnev had to change his tone. He had to promise that he would put things in order in Temirtau and would punish the culprits.

In the summer of 1959, the discontent that had been contained for so long, finally erupted. The young people who had come from all over the country came face to face with the administrative-command system that cared little about ordinary human needs. The factory was being raised at lightning speed while the workers lived in tents and hastily assembled barracks. Often there were not enough protective outer garments to go around. People were particularly weary of the poor water supply. Usually the workers would not have any water until lunch time, and then it was not clear and had an unhealthy odour. The situation with food was terrible. Everyone's patience ended when they learned that a large amount of meat, Siberian dumplings, and fruit had been buried in the ground at the food warehouse. Supplies of concrete, and other construction materials became scarce, so the workers lost money when they had nothing to work with.

On July 29, a crowd of thousands of bricklayers, concrete layers and assemblers who had stopped working gathered on a square by the headquarters of the construction site to complain to the management. The angry workers saw that nobody wanted to talk to them and decided to take justice into their own hands. They tore the locks off grocery stores and carried away vegetables and potatoes. Some of them even managed to get at the vodka. The most enterprising among them took bales of consumer goods home. That night troops entered the city and shooting began. People were arrested and a curfew was declared. Later the "ringleaders" were tried.

Gradually life went back to normal. When we returned the blast furnace was still not operating, and so we were given other jobs. I had quickly to master the techniques of concrete laying. We worked day shifts and night shifts because the concrete always had to be hot, so there could be not interruptions in the work process. Our living conditions were so bad I prefer not to remember. We were moved from damp and dirty basement accommodations to an unheated dormitory where we kept warm by sleeping in twos on iron cots covered by mattresses. There was no place to even hang out our clothes to dry. We kept our canvas work clothes out in the frost because it was easier to put them on when they were frozen than when they were wet and heavy. We had to carry our main tools to work every morning—sledge hammer and a wide shovel. I would not even recall all this if it had been a construction project during the times of Kuznetskstroi, and not in recent history. There may be some justification for the sacrifices people made for industrialization in the early days of Soviet government, but there is no explanation for the indifference to people demonstrated in the sixties and subsequent decades. We mixed up the end and the means, and turned people into an extension of an all-devouring economic machine that demanded more and more of human beings while giving nothing in return. Maybe Andrei Platonov was right when he looked at these "great construction projects" and said what we were really doing was cheerfully digging a monstrous pit for ourselves.

It is also necessary to mention another characteristic of many national Young Communist League construction projects, a characteristic that I hope is past history. At first we had to work the same shift with convicts. In all fairness I have to say that they never did anything bad to us. On the contrary, they showed genuine concern. For instance, they would take some strange breaks when they would pass a cigarette around. After a few puffs someone might start crying, and another one start laughing. Finally, curiosity got the best of us and we asked them if we could have a try. But when they asked us our age they gave a quick no. It was only later that I realized they had been smoking marijuana, or something like it.

I am beginning to understand many things only now. For instance, how genuine youthful enthusiasm was exploited shamefully. In those days it all seemed quite normal. I remember that in 1962, when I was addressing the 11th Congress of the Young Communist League of Kazakhstan, I passionately urged people to come to Temirtau. Young workers were leaving because there were not enough young women. My speech got a big ovation.

On July 3, 1960, the blast furnace went into operation. It was the only one then in Central Asia and Kazakhstan. This day went down in history as the birthday of the Karaganda Metallurgical Plant. There were big parades, rallies, speeches. Afterwards, life went back to normal, and for thousands of people from all over the country, it was anything but cheerful. The residential area was not close to the plant, and no one gave any thought to how we were supposed to get to work. We spent two hours simply going to and from work. The dormitory was cold, we never got enough sleep, and survived only because we were young and strong. There were not even any recreational activities organized. The only entertainment people had was big fights—Dnepropetrovsk against Odessa, Sverdlovsk agains Cherepovets, Gomel against people from somewhere else. Every day there were murders and other big troubles.

Such experiences usually leave their mark. If it had not been for our older friends who taught us common sense, more of the young people would have had their lives ruined from the start. These older men taught their lessons without us really noticing. They might mumble some approval if we deserved it, but the rest of the time they instructed us quietly, by their own example.

I will never forget Boris Yagovitov. When we were transferred to the furnace, he was our team leader. When people ask me what I think a real Bolshevik is, he is the first person who comes to mind. I joined the party because of the example he set in his attitude to life, and commitment to his work. He gave me his recommendation. I joined the party completely convinced that this organization guarantees people justice and is a force against lies and vices. Yagovitov was not a well educated man (he finished the fourth grade), but he knew the steel industry better than any engineer. For instance, he could determine the chemical content of metal just by looking at it. He had come to Temirtau from the Magnitogorsk Steel Plant together with his family. I remember when one of our young workers would lose heart, he would always cheer them up, assuring them they would someday be good steel workers. Of course the old steel workers used some methods that would seem shocking. For instance, the first pay day was also the initiation day. In those days there was no such thing as a city without a market place or a market place without a beer stand. My turn came, I remember, after the night shift. I was supposed to take the whole team to have a beer, all eight men. Although I was already twenty, I had never had any wine. In the village where my father lived it was unthinkable to drink, and at the vocational school there was no such practice.

Conversation about the beer parlour was short:

"Go and get it."

"How many?" I asked.

"Eight bottles. Got enough money?"

"I can take care of it myself."

I went to the store, bought eight bottles of vodka and set them on the table. I remember we were all tired after working all night in a rolling shop. We got some glasses and a mug of beer for each person. When everyone had plenty to drink they started egging me on:

"So what's wrong with you, just standing there watching us? You have to start sometime".

They poured me half a glass. I finished it off in one gulp and drank it down with beer. That's the last thing I remember. I don't know when I passed out. When I woke up I was lying on a wide bed, the sheets were white and starched. I had a soft blanket covering me, and my head was on a huge feather pillow. It turned out I was in Yagovitov's home, and had slept there for a whole twenty-four hours. His wife, Maria Vasilievna, brought me a huge bowl of steaming dumplings, and Boris took out a bottle of vodka.

"I understand you, young man, I won't make you drink. But I think you should have just a little bit."

That's how they made workers out of us.

When you talk about your childhood and youth, you continually stressed the role your family and relatives played in your development. Anyone would agree that healthy family traditions are the foundation of a healthy nation or society. In this context I would like to talk about the eternal problem of fathers and sons, and the generation gap. Has this gap become irreparable?

For decades we tried to create new traditions artificially and introduce them in all spheres of life. Presumably all our customs that had developed over the centuries were taking us backward, were resisting social progress, especially religious traditions. In our fight against "backwardness and patriarchal ways" we tore up our ethnic roots, and often committed outrages against the age-old experience of generations before us. Even today there are still many political and public leaders, afraid to be labeled as conservatives, who advocate dubious innovations accepted by the young. They are skeptical about such sacred ethnic traditions as respect for elders, patriotism, and love of country.

I believe that healthy conservatism does not stop progress. On the contrary, it facilitates it. Japan is a good example. It reached the heights of scientific and technological progress by relying on its conservative traditions. I saw this phenomenon in South Korea. In my opinion the Kazakhs developed wonderful traditions and customs long ago. I mentioned some of them already when I talked about my childhood. An important Kazakh tradition is the preservation of bonds between relatives. All the relatives gather together to share in the joys or sorrows of one of them. I talked about how children are taught to respect adults and to honour women. The oldest son in a family has a responsibility for younger brothers and sisters. A family with elders living in the home was considered fortunate. The youngest son was supposed to remain in the home even after starting his own family. This home, called the shanrak, in which the youngest son, father, mother, grandmother and grandfather lived, was the main one for the rest of the family. Such traditions are conducive to raising children and shaping the character of young people.

In my opinion religious customs are also important if they promote kindness and humaneness. Until recently if a communist participated in a religious ceremony in connection with a death or a birth this person could be accused of anti-party behaviour. That is how absurd things got.

So it is no wonder that young people don't think much of our opinions and principles. They sometimes even ridicule us. We are certainly seeing a generation gap. It will take a long time to fill this gap because we have spent too much time destroying things with our own hands.

I don't want to repeat banalities about the role of the family, school, and the need to build a qualitatively new system of upbringing and education. Naturally, this has to be done in a fundamental way. But we have to remember that we cannot do this with slogans and new "moral codes."

I think the main road to moral rejuvenation is by resurrecting a sense of healthy pride in one's nationality and traditions. I view this process in the broadest terms, because I am talking about reviving the economy, culture, and the political system. Perestroika has started us on this road, and we have taken many big steps forward. For the first time since Soviet government was established freedom of conscience is not just a declaration but a reality. At the same time I think that many cultural figures understand the concept of new thinking rather oddly. In print and electronic media, and other channels of communication I see that we have adopted too many dubious "values" from the western, "civilized" world. I don't want to go into the issues of mass culture or youth subcultures. All I want to say is that we should not indiscriminately latch onto everything abroad that may not be so welcome there either. I think that many disturbing tendencies among the young—egotistical individualism, license to do anything they want, and degeneracy—have been borrowed or "imported."

In reading your biography one wonders whether leaders are born or are trained by life to be organizers.

I never really gave that any serious thought. However I do think that many leadership abilities are inborn. All bureaucratic character references say that a person "has good organizational abilities." However, to be a good leader it is not enough to be a talented organizer. A leader has to have the trust and recognition of the people. In life we often meet wonderful and talented professionals who know their field, but they are not always able to manage others, unite and lead them.

I was never ambitious about taking on management positions. However from childhood I always had an inner sense of self-worth that kept me from being "mediocre." For example, I always wanted to be the best student. I think this is only natural for anyone with self-respect. Without self-respect a person cannot get anywhere in life. In my case I always ended up in some leadership body. In the upper grades of secondary school I was elected a member of the school's student committee, and was always an activist in the Young Communist League at school and in the district.

Throughout my life I have dealt with a large number of people in leadership positions at various levels. I noticed that many of them were athletic, were physically strong and well-coordinated. I think this has a lot to do with the fact that in childhood the people who tend to be looked up to by their peers are those who have outstanding physical or other qualities. That was the case with Ryspanov, whom I already mentioned. Physical strength probably played the decisive role in the struggle for leadership within the group.

Since you mentioned "struggle for leadership" I would like to point out that we have always been taught that struggle for power is characteristic only of the West, that in a socialist democracy all people inevitably take the place in life that they are qualified for.

Of course that is not the case. We are seeing an overt, and sometimes fierce struggle for power in politics today. What counts are the goals of this struggle. If people aspiring to positions of power are driven by personal ambition and self interest we should not only resist them but struggle against them. However we must only use constitutional parliamentary methods.

CHAPTER THREE

Seniority at the Furnace

Unfortunately there is a tendency in our country to envy "big money," This is understandable, but sometimes such envy is indiscriminate. After all there are two kinds of "big money," the kind that is thrown around on conspicuous consumption, and the kind that is saved up to help children start their adult lives or to give aging parents a decent standard of living. The sources of this money can also be different.

Within half a year after I started working on the blast furnace I was making 4,500 a month. In those days, 1960, that was an unbelievable income for a twenty-year-old. I sent 2,000 to my father every month. When I later found out that he did not spend a kopeck of that money on himself, I felt a lump in my throat because I knew that he was barely making a living. If he did spend any of the money it was only on the children, on my brothers. When he received the first money order from me he called together the whole village, and said, "You see, my Sultan is earning money." When I was declared an exceptional worker and my photograph appeared in the Kazakhstan Pravda (I was wearing a hat!), my father invited the whole village to a big banquet. I don't think fame means anything compared with the elation experienced in making relatives happy and satisfied.

I started out making cast iron, and later I was made the fourth furnaceman. What kind of work does a furnaceman do? It is toilsome labour, because the scrap has to be cut, and moved with a heavy shovel. The temperature in there is about 2000 degrees Celsius, and the atmosphere full of gas and dust. These men have a terrible job. There is no time to complain or take a break. You have to rely on yourself. When your skills are inadequate you can often allow the metal to cool off which causes accidents. It is necessary to get right into the flame with an asbestos coat in order to pull out the broken machinery. During a shift you have to drink half a bucket of salt water to compensate for all the sweat. After work it takes half an hour in a cold shower to return to normal. In the summer it is also hot outside, as high as 35 degrees Celsius. The workers were always exhausted from the heat, their muscles never got a chance to relax. Some had constant nose bleeds. Not everyone had the same stamina. A few could not handle the strain, so they went home.

I remember when my father came to visit and see what my job was like. He went with me to the night shift. As fate would have it we had a big accident and I was involved in the cleanup. He watched that whole ordeal, and the next morning he tried to persuade me to leave: "Why are you torturing yourself? I was an orphan at the age of three and saw a lot in my life, but I never experienced such hell. Give it up."

Much later, when I visited steel plants in other countries I was both proud of my basic skills and at the same time I was upset, especially in South Korea when I saw blast furnaces designed by the Japanese. The working conditions were completely different—everything was mechanised, the floor was clean and orderly. It is all the more troubling to think that our steel workers and miners can boast the world's largest output, but their labour still requires superhuman physical and moral qualities.

In those days we worked with people who had been in the steel industry for years. They were invited from the Urals, Ukraine, and West Siberia. They were offered a lot of money for relocation, and apartments right away. They watched as some of our young men were carried out of the shops on stretchers, and shrugged: "How can you teach them this job; all they're good for is herding sheep."

Frankly I was terribly offended, but I do not hold anything against those workers. First, such attitudes were usually due to poor education; some workers had finished only three or four grades. Second, they were not expressing an ethnic bias but professional superiority. This is common among people in dangerous professions because in their opinion the work is not for ordinary mortals. Later I realized that these were the men who had made us steel workers.

At that time, however, I swore to myself that I would rather die than let anyone say that about me. That is how I survived. Many of my friends also met the challenge and became highly skilled steel workers, for example, Tulegen Yusupov and Bulat Karimov.

Those who remained gradually grew accustomed to the work. I progressed in my skills rapidly. I soon regained the classification I got in vocational school—the eighth. Within half a year I became the second furnaceman. Any steel worker knows that it takes a minimum of ten years to manage the process and the work crew at a furnace. It is also important to know that in a work crew of six to eight people it was rare to have two or three who were of the same nationality. In our group I was the only Kazakh. In addition to me there was a Tatar, a Russian, a Ukrainian . . .

People were judged not by the ethnic background, but by the way they worked. In this environment it was easy to see who was always ready to lend a helping hand, who was prepared to take responsibilities, and volunteer for the hardest job. Such people earned special respect and were models for others.

No one compelled me to join the Communist Party. That was a phenomenon that came later when workers had to be coaxed into applying for the party at the same time that long waiting lists of technicians and engineers developed for party membership. When I joined I was not thinking of big career opportunities or benefits.

As I already said, I simply saw such good examples to follow. The communists were always the best workers. Besides, everyone knew that the party organization could make demands on a shop foreman or any other manager.

Today all communists are often asked to repent, as a herd, so to speak. Appeals are sometimes made to test party members. It is as if we have a new kind of "enemy of the people." What can I say about this? I think that repentance is something very personal, and depends on one's conscience. Coercion does not do any good. Besides, how can we blame millions of communists who believed in the ideals of justice and lived by those principles? No one ever stops to think what might have happened to all of us, to our history if it had not been for this healthy core that could not be broken either by the Stalin purges or any other harsh trials. If it had not been for millions of such people in the party it is hard to say when profound reforms would have begun.

I joined the party knowing full well that I would gain nothing but additional responsibilities. However, as I found out, not everyone understood this responsibility in the same way. I was truly shocked when the city party committee gave me a strong reprimand and entered it in my records. This is a serious matter for any party member, but especially for a young communist. This threatened to leave an indelible mark against me for the rest of my life, which was just beginning. How could I prove myself to everyone along the way who would see this reprimand in my records?

One day I was asked to see the first secretary of the city party committee, Lazar Katkov. By that time I was very active in community affairs, was a delegate to the republican and national congresses of the Young Communist League, and was elected head of the party organization of my shop and member of the Central Committee of the Young Communist League. However I could not imagine being elected first secretary of the city committee of the Young Communist League. I was not even thinking about a political career and giving up my job as a steel worker.

When the offer was made my first thought, frankly, was that a YCL secretary made one-third the salary of a steel worker, and what was more important, I would lose my seniority as a steel worker. Young people don't think about the distant future and retirement. Youth seems eternal. However, to a steel worker seniority was very important and certainly was an influential factor in our thinking. Seniority was not only a matter of professional pride, but the benefits were significant and the retirement age was substantially lower than average. Older steel workers realized the consequences of working with hot steel, and had no illusions about inexhaustible health. Incidentally, I had seven years of seniority.

Naturally when I had that meeting in the city party committee I did not say anything about salary or seniority; after all, a party member was supposed to care only about "higher interests." My answer, though, was a definite no. That was when I learned what people in Temirtau meant when they said that you don't fool with Comrade Katkov. He gave me a day to think it over. The next day the conversation went basically the same way. I had to listen to a short lecture about party discipline, and about how I ought to think about my future. I can't say that I wasn't vacillating at all. However I had an uncontrollable desire to resist such strong pressure. When I said that I had thought it over carefully, Katkov stood up abruptly and said, "Remember, you won't get a third chance."

I was wrong to think that this was the end of the matter. Two weeks later someone else was elected secretary of the YCL committee and I was summoned to the bureau of the city party committee. The head of the organizational department read me the verdict in a prepared statement: "For refusing . . . for political immaturity . . . for demonstrating indifference . . ." The secretary of the plant's party committee and the director who were also members of the party bureau were not able to defend me. Comrade Katkov did not fool around: "A strong reprimand in his record to serve as an example to others."

I don't know what possessed me to go to the city telegraph office, which was across the street from the city committee, and call the first secretary of the Young Communist League, Sergei Pavlov. A few days later there was a meeting of the regional party bureau at which my reprimand was lifted and Katkov was officially criticized for the wrong approach to selecting personnel. He was never able to forgive me for this. Once we met by a blast furnace. He took me aside and told me he would never forgive me for what I did.

Thank God we never crossed paths again. Katkov was assigned to the Dzhambul Region where he was promoted to second secretary of the regional party committee. However that incident left a deep impression on me. It did not shake my belief in justice, but it did raise serious doubts about taking everything at face value. Later there were many occasions when I clashed openly with the command style of management and the army-like discipline in the party which until recently was generally accepted as normal. The hardest thing was to explain anything to people who thought it was sinful to disagree even slightly with the "general course." Appeals to common sense were often met with the reply, "I am a soldier of the party." A soldier is not supposed to discuss the forbidden. Sometimes I would think to myself that if the top leaders considered themselves soldiers, then what were ordinary communists? I think that leaders such as Katkov were victims of this army-like "soldier" mentality. It was inconceivable to him that a communist could refuse such an important assignment by the city committee.

This mentality also morally corrupted party officials. Behind the strict framework of strangely understood party ethics, hypocrisy and corruption were common. I cannot say, or rather I do not have the right to say that these phenomena were widespread. The vast majority of party members that I have known closely are truly devoted to their work, and are certainly honest people. Sometimes, however, especially at the high leadership level, I have seen such degenerate human beings that it is mind-boggling to contemplate where they came from. After all, these are people with power over other people's lives. I often recall terrible incidents from my own experience when efforts were made to compromise me, high-handed leaders were forced to give evidence to the investigation. I was bombarded with phone calls from anonymous blackmailers who threatened reprisals against my loved ones. Once a merciless creature called my wife and said I was killed in an automobile accident. This is not to mention the hundreds of anonymous complaints filed at various levels, including the Politburo. It is hard to recall everything. Incidentally, this was happening during the period of perestroika.

I must admit that ultimately I headed the YCL city committee in Temirtau. The new party secretary, Nikolai Davydov, who replaced Katkov, called me to his office and said: "I know about the conversations you had with Katkov. Still I would like to ask you to work in the city party committee as the head of the heavy industry department. You will be dealing with your plant, so you will not be leaving the steel industry."

I went back to the shop and talked to my friends. Their advice was, "Go ahead and work there, then come back. They won't eat you. And you'll probably gain experience. Besides, you shouldn't test fate a second time." They were right; I did not stay long in the city party committee. But since the new head of the city YCL did not "make the grade," I ended up in his job.

By that time I already had considerable experience and self-assurance to take me through the storms in life. I had a college education. A few men and myself from the shop were sponsored by the plant at the Karaganda Polytechnic Institute. The plant paid our stipends.

In those days Nikita Khrushchev was reorganizing higher education to make it as relevant as possible to industry. Despite the long hours, I had a relatively easy time studying. If we were on the night shift we went to lectures in the day, and vice versa. Every month we spent several days on lectures, seminars and laboratory work. We had that convenient schedule for a year. The next two years we were full-time students, until the metallurgy department of the polytechnic institute opened a branch on the site of the steel plant. That is where we finally earned our degrees.

The most memorable event of those days was when I met my future wife, Sarah. This occurred right by the blast furnace after an accident. When there is an accident and the metal spills over onto the ground, the workers do not leave until they clean up all the scrap metal and restart the railway transport. That is a strict rule, no matter what time of day or night—you have to clean up your own mess. I had been on my feet for nearly twenty-four hours, was covered with soot, with only my eyes and teeth shining when I met this young woman. She was on duty that night at the electrical substation and came over to see what the situation was with the furnace. Not long afterwards we had a big wedding sponsored by the YCL, since I was an outstanding worker and activist. As was customary in these cases, we were presented with the keys to our own apartment.

However, when we went to the assigned address, we saw that construction had barely begun on the five-storey building with eighty apartments. After the wedding we had to live with a friend who had a tiny one-bedroom apartment. He lived there with his wife, two children, and their grandmother. We spent our wedding night in the same room with Grandma. That was unforgettable.

Since then my wife and I have lived together happily for nearly three decades. We have three daughters. The older two are married, and the youngest is still in school. Perhaps I wouldn't get into the subject of my family, and these personal matters, if it weren't for one problem that doesn't give me any rest. Recently my youngest daughter Aliya came home from music school, and asked: "Why do the teachers call all the girls by name, but they always call me by my last name?" What could I say? That her older sisters had the same problems in Alma-Ata when I became secretary of the Central Committee? They often came home in tears after hearing the teachers say, "Don't forget that you're Nazarbayev's daughter," or "That's Nazarbayev's daughter." People seem to think that the children of leaders don't have their own opinions or their own abilities. God forbid if they act like children and get into trouble! Getting dressed for school is a whole ordeal, because they know that everything they wear is a subject for discussion. Perhaps this is because our people are generally unsophisticated. But there are some grounds for the stereotypical thinking that if you are related to a top leader you must reap the benefits and live accordingly. I don't know if this is the situation in other countries. I have travelled a lot, but haven't seen anything similar.

Incidentally, the first time I had any experience in international relations (now I see it was rather dubious) was at the World Youth Festival held in Helsinki where I was a member of the Soviet delegation. Our delegation wanted to focus on the discussion of the advantages of socialism over capitalism. We were given thorough preparations for these discussions by the Central Committee of the Young Communist League and the Central YCL School. As a result we were convinced that in all capitalist countries the oppressor bourgeoisie constantly bled dry the working class and that the progressive young people in Western countries longed to throw off this terrible yoke. So we were surprised to find that most of our counterparts were much more concerned about the communist threat that supposedly emanated from our country. They thought we were ready to force communist ideas on people everywhere we could at the point of a gun. As you can see, the ideologists and propagandists of both worlds were the same.

The main question that was posed to us constantly was, "What do you have in the Soviet Union?" We eagerly explained that money wasn't everything, that we lived for the future, that we lived in a just society, that we were building a new society not divided into rich and poor, white and black.

I remember a meeting with students from Brooklyn College when one of the young women, Karen Lagodo, said to me: "You're probably the son of some big communist to have come to this festival." I resorted to the only sure proof I had and showed her my hands that were covered with a thick layer of calluses. Amazed by what she saw, she felt my rough hands with her delicate fingers.

In many ways we were helped by the fact that Yuri Gagarin, the world's first cosmonaut, was in our delegation. His simplicity and charm invariably won appreciation. The welcome he was given at the Senate Square in Helsinki reflected a show of warmth that had not been offered to us for a long time.

My friends and fellow steel workers were wise in advising me to take that job. Gradually I gained experience in dealing with all types of people, from ordinary workers to ministers. Admittedly, that experience did not come easy. In some ways it was like building seniority at the blast furnace. Most importantly, it helped me stay thoroughly involved in my natural element, the steel industry, without which I could not imagine my life.

I realize I can be criticized for being too proud of my original profession, nevertheless I want to quote something said to me by Vassili Akulintsev. During the early seventies he was the first secretary of the Karaganda Regional Committee of the Communist Party and was an extraordinarily broad-minded and cultured man who was amazingly competent in a diverse range of issues. In my opinion he was the model of an educated party official. He would often say that anyone who did not understand ferrous metallurgy could not be considered cultured or educated.

Judge for yourself. The metallurgical process begins with mining. First it is necessary to extract the ore and coal, then the ore has to be turned into a concentrate, and the coal has to become coke. Coke production at a steel plant is the whole chemical process from A to Z. Manufacturing cast iron and steel is also an entire science involving the most complex technologies. Without boring the reader with a lot of details I would just like to draw an overall picture of the Karaganda plant to show how huge it was. The railway on the plant's grounds accounted for nearly 400 kilometers of steel tracks. The plant maintained 1,500 vehicles. The repair shops turned over 30–40 million rubles annually. We generated all our own power. In addition to all this, the construction work was worth 120 million rubles a year, and two huge agricultural areas required millions of rubles of investments. So Akulintsev's comment was not far off the mark.

As second secretary of the city party committee in charge of industry and capital construction, I did not sit in the office pushing a pencil. I spent day and night at the construction sites of the steel plant, supervising the political activities. I wasn't always sure whether I was working together with the manager or instead of him. My pace was dizzying; I could be at a blast furnace after an accident, at the converter, writing out schedules late into the night, submitting hundreds of different legal documents, organizing weekend overtime, overseeing the transportation of concrete, metal and equipment. Every day I met with dozens and hundreds of people. People came around the clock to construction headquarters with the most diverse and sometimes unexpected problems and requests—a foreman might be threatening to take a crew off the job if the supply of concrete wasn't more regular, or a worker's wife might want us to influence her alcoholic husband to stop drinking.

I suppose we are the only country in the world that establishes various political institutions for just about any reason. Life was inconceivable without such organizations that oversaw the minutest details of any undertaking, whether in industry, or in efforts to fight crime or develop entertainment facilities in neighbourhoods. Why did we need all these organizations? Is it because it was really necessary to have strong centralized organizations that focus their efforts and resources on the most important enterprises? Or is it because our government and industrial management structures were inadequate and unable to plan and organize work? Looking back, I tend to lean toward the latter reason.

The two years that I spent as the head of the plant's construction project seemed to be one unending workday. I had plenty of energy for the job since I was young and realized that this undertaking was one of the biggest in those days, and much of what we were doing was being accomplished for the first time in our country. For instance, the Karaganda plant was the first to build a 250 ton converter, 600 ton open-hearth furnaces, the most powerful slabbing unit and rolled metal unit.

Not a month went by without visits from the large national ministries in charge of ferrous metallurgy, heavy construction, special assembly work, heavy engineering, and electrical technical industry. Every quarter we also had visits from A. N. Tikhonov, first deputy of A. N. Kosygin, Chairman of the USSR Council of Ministers. This is not to mention officials from the Central Committee of the Communist Party of the Soviet Union, the Central Committee of the Communist Party of Kazakhstan, and the Regional Committee of the Communist Party. They inspected the construction project thoroughly, and always had some advice and admonishments. The worst times were when we were up against a deadline before a big holiday, like May Day, November 7, the New Year, or the opening of a party congress. Thousands of people were taken off less urgent jobs to finish a project on time. We were put under tremendous pressure. The national and republican officials cared only about completing the job. Afterwards medals were sent by the boxfuls. I remember how we had to complete one of our chemical plants no matter what it took so that the head of the trust, A. G. Korkin, a delegate to the 24th party congress, could report on the plant's completion. He made the report on time, but on the first day of the congress one of the galleries collapsed.

The builders were not at all to blame. In extremely difficult conditions they worked as hard as was humanly possible; they had a strong sense of responsibility. The others involved were the designers and the "campaign leaders". As a result of their "efforts" big changes had to be made and the people's money was thrown to the wind. When anything went wrong they pointed the finger at the builders and steel workers.

I don't remember any conversation with top visiting officials about the living conditions of the steel workers or the builders. No such conversations ever occurred simply because no one thought about the people, about their housing, childcare, food, or consumer goods. Yet these problems grew like a snowball rolling down a hill, and resulted in work stoppages once the plant was operating. The rush jobs were a big reason for the problems because something was always overlooked that kept us from producing the kind of steel that was needed. The workers were under considerable stress, because there were so many accidents, they never had weekends off, and their wages were decreased catastrophically during these periods. There was a thirty percent turnover in workers. The plant was not efficient.

As soon as the plant started work there was chaos in the management. Shop foremen, leading engineers and directors were replaced, one after another. It was during that time, in 1972, that I was appointed secretary of the plant's committee. There were 30,000 workers; 2,500 of them were in the Communist Party. So that was when my real work in the party began. It was not exactly a good beginning. The month before I started, a new director took over. He was Oleg Tishchenko, and had come from the Urals, from the Chelyabinsk Steel Plant. That first year he and I made a mess of everything. The newspapers increasingly ran stories criticizing the plant, and often they mentioned our names.

I think we both caught equal fire. The secretary of the party committee was just as responsible for the plant as the director. In many cases, for instance, as far as the Central Committee was concerned, the secretary's responsibility was even greater. In those days special demands were put on such people; the consequences of failure were unpredictable. Of course, they were protected from attacks from officials lower down the hierarchy. It's simpler when you know from whom to expect attacks. I always speak well of Tishchenko. He had his weaknesses; for instance, he tended to drink too much. We all have our faults. But he worked selflessly. He distinguished between primary and secondary issues, and always had a clear plan of action. We were never diplomatically polite with each other, but we got along right away, and promised to coordinate our efforts, since we shared responsibility equally.

From the outset we had to deal with big problems. It took more than one year to pull the plant out of its quagmire. Looking at old Pravdas from 1977, I found an article I had written about the plant, and how backward it was considered. I won't go into the problems that I attempted to analyze. In my opinion what's interesting today is the brief commentary by the editorial board: "Recently the party committee of the Karaganda Steel Plant approved the example set by the work team headed by T. Adam-Yusupov. The team decided to utilize the designed capacity of the blast furnace ahead of schedule and ensure thousands of tons of output beyond planned targets. The collective in the blast furnace shop supported the initiators and made high commitments for the first year of the tenth five-year plan. But they did not even manage to reach the targets of the state plan. Even before that the steel workers, following the example of I. Abdirov, decided to work for the goal of producing high quality steel every shift. Throughout the plant the workers competed to put out the best possible steel. Despite this, defective steel is produced in many shops."

I have cited those comments in full because I believe they reflect the nature of the times that we now refer to as the period of stagnation. In this article we see the familiar reference to big plans and common failures.

In this context I recall another instance which was atypical but rather interesting and instructive. In 1973, our plant was visited by Vladimir Dolgikh, a newly appointed secretary of the Communist Party Central Committee. The steel workers could see right away that this man knew what he was talking about. It's no wonder, because by that time he had a lot of experience working as the director of the Norilsk Steel Plant, and secretary of the Krasnoyarsk Territory Committee of the Communist Party. The director and I took him around to the various shops and construction sites in three or four days. As secretary of the party committee I told him all about our catastrophic housing problems, lack of recreational and other important facilities, about the high worker turnover, and about the flaws in our plant that required additional capital and the return of builders who had been sent off to other sites.

Three weeks after he left a delegation of fifty people arrived from the Central Committee. They were supposed to write a report entitled "About the Efforts of the Party Committee of the Karanganda Steel Plant to Strengthen Discipline and Create a Stable Collective." I figured I had really done myself in that time. It's interesting to mention what the members of the commission ultimately said at the end of the visit. It was commonly understood in those days that if a factory was reaching its targets the party committee was doing a good job, all the communists were wonderful, competition was working well, the meeting agendas were fine, and work with individuals was constructive. The commission was amazed that in our case it was just the opposite. Everywhere they looked at the plant there were problems. But no matter how hard they tried to find fault with the work of the party organization, they were unsuccessful.

Right after I became secretary of the party committee I think I made the right decision by relying completely on the dedicated rank and file party members in the shops. I saw over and over again how five to ten percent of the real dedicated party members in a team could unite the others and get things moving in the shop. It was only with their help that we were able to keep the collective from falling apart at the plant, and improve work discipline. Incidentally, I am convinced that now, no matter how much we seek new, progressive methods of economic management, we won't get anywhere without strict work discipline at every enterprise. When Tishchenko and I started working together, the plant was in a state of near anarchy. Absenteeism was high, workers were continually late, and as a result skills of the workers and engineers deteriorated and equally declined. When we talk about the role of the communists who were mobilized to wage an uncompromising battle for better discipline, it is necessary to point out that in those days there was democracy and direct criticism of the managers, especially in the rank and file party organizations in the shops. Party meetings and conferences did not go smoothly, especially when it was time to elect a party bureau, the party committee and secretaries. There was no such thing as "anyone but me." I remember when a suggestion was made to appoint an assistant secretary of the party committee a man who was the head of the propaganda department in the city party committee and a capable, honest, conscientious person. But the conference delegates were adamantly against this choice because they felt ideologists at the plant had to know all about the steel industry. The first secretaries of the regional and city party committees who had recommended this man could do nothing about it. So there were alternative candidates in those days too; the workers weren't particularly concerned about what the bosses thought.

Members of the party committee, the director and myself tried to establish good relations with everyone. For instance, we spent the New Year with the shifts that were scheduled to work. We came to them with flowers and went home with them. We had frank conversations over tea with the skilled workers, team leaders, and engineers (there were 3,200 of them in the steel plant). In fact many of them, because of the constant backups, accidents and overtime, stopped thinking effectively and ceased to be good engineers. That's why at first they practically had to be forced to study, to keep up their own skills. We organized courses, and collected engineering libraries. We kept track of the books, magazines, and articles the engineers were reading.

Generally the people we relied on did not let us down. I often remember the period when we demanded their total self-sacrifice. I suppose this is why I can't agree with the blanket criticism of the Party and the assertions that the party played only a reactionary role in the past. I can't help thinking that no one, under any circumstances, can get me to turn my back on those people. However, all our efforts to pull our plant out of the quagmire came up against insurmountable obstacles. At times we felt that we were fighting some invisible but real force. The plant continued to flounder.

By then I had to go to Moscow and report to the Secretariate of the Central Committee. A department in the Central Committee prepared us for the various unexpected questions that might be raised. I was told, "Tomorrow you're going to meet with Mikhail Suslov." I figured I was going to be dismissed from my job. I wasn't particularly upset because I knew I could always return to the floor.

You said that we are not always in a position to choose the people who surround us, and we even make friends in strange ways. What are the principles that guide you in solving personnel problems?

Yes, it's true that you can't always choose the people you work with. But you have to be discriminating when you choose your friends. You have to be able to distinguish between real friends and ordinary co-workers.

My experience has shown me that relations between people in industries are more spontaneous and open. Thirty years ago I started my adult life together with steel workers. To this day I have the same simple and sincere relations with them. In the upper echelons of power, of course, everything is much more complex. The higher the position, the harder it is to make friends and develop close relationships. To be frank, opportunistic considerations affect these relations. Many people are obviously fawning.

God forbid that a person gets trapped into friendship this way. These are just fair weather friends. Many times in my life I have experienced the bitter pain of disappointment in people I thought were my friends. You put your trust in someone, he supports you in words, but in deeds he jumps over to the other side of the barricades. Everywhere we can see people who used to be considered our comrades, but now they've changed colours because the wind is blowing the other way. Real friends are tested over time, and they don't care what post you hold, what job you do, what benefit they get from knowing you. In my opinion selflessness is the primary criterion of genuine friendship.

What can I say about the main principles in choosing personnel at this complex stage of our society? First of all it is necessary to be realistic—most people have been trained in an administrative-command system. But this does not mean that all of them are carrying the old baggage of work methods that are no longer relevant. In some places "revolutionary" changes have been made, and the entire management has been replaced with younger people. This thoughtless approach is to blame for incompetence at many leadership bodies. We cannot afford to ignore the vast experience accumulated by managers and political leaders. At the same time, of course, we can only depend on those who support perestroika, radical economic reforms. Our problem is that we don't really have qualified people for these changes. That is why we have to train ourselves and at the same time prepare younger people. Most importantly we have to give complete support to people who show initiative, who are sincerely trying to reform our economy and our whole way of life.

According to you, the turning point in the party began long ago, at any rate, several years before perestroika. In fact some alarming phenomena were already evident. For instance, workers were not anxious to join the party, formalism replaced vibrant party activities. What was the reason for these negative tendencies?

You may remember that sometime during the seventies there was much talk in the upper echelons of the party about the unity of words and deeds. It sounded very hypocritical because these people should have been taking their own advice. The top leadership of the party increasingly separated itself from the rank and file by creating the cult of personality of Leonid Brezhnev and by taking advantage of the privileges in being close to the leader. Essentially these people became indifferent to the affairs of the party, to its core — the rank and file organizations. Well managed vertical structures were needed to keep things calm at the top. This was the orientation of the system of strict party discipline in the apparatuses. The numerous resolutions on improving inner party work were just for show. That is why the activities of the lower party bodies were increasingly meant for show. The party's prestige rapidly declined because no one expected anything from party leaders but formalistic reports and dogmatic rhetoric. People began to join the party not out of sincere convictions. Some, mainly workers, were persuaded to join, in order to boost the percentage of working class members. Others, the intelligentsia, joined for the sake of their careers. No one believed anymore the lofty assertions that the party gave no benefits, that communists had only one privilege, to be in the forefront where life was harder. As a result there were increasingly fewer people with the militant qualities of those Bolsheviks whom I knew when I started working. It is no wonder that when the sixth article of the USSR Constitution was abolished, the party was not only incapable of taking the offensive, but could not even wage a proper defense.

As you said, you got into political work against your own wishes, not because you planned to do so. Perhaps this is a naive question, but still I would like to know what you would do if you had to choose all over again?

You seem to realize yourself that your question is somewhat rhetorical in relation to the current stage of my life. However, I admit that deep in my heart I am still dedicated to steel work. You've probably already realized that my initial profession gave me more than just a job skill and experience. Yes, there was a time when I could not imagine my life without the steel industry. But life has a way of doing what it wants. Now I have behind me a long political career. Political work enabled me to develop other potential. But real satisfaction comes not from having an impact on important processes under way now in the republic or in the country as a whole. A political career is primarily hard work, and believe me, knowing that I bear colossal responsibility does not ensure peace of mind. Only one thing can give moral satisfaction—the realization that you understand the needs and the desires of your people, that you can express them, and that you have the people's support. However you cannot allow your price to be inflated. We all know the consequences of being too self satisfied.

What I think about most is how to justify the people's trust. I see only one way to accomplish this—by forging steadily ahead with perestroika and bringing others along with you. There is no other way to improve the lives of the people who are tired of promises and who deserve a better life.

CHAPTER FOUR

A Vicious Circle

In recent years, when social thought in this country finally became unfettered, all of us were able openly to express our opinion of the current changes, predictions for the future, and, naturally, the experiences of our past. This phenomenon is not only natural, but necessary for the improvement of society, especially if we don't want to see our intellectual and spiritual life suppressed again within the framework of totalitarian ideas. It doesn't bother me that people are expressing diametrically opposed opinions and irreconcilable positions. This is quite normal.

But one habit in these discussions bothers me very much. I have noticed that whether the debate is about economic ideas and programmes, about the prospects for social development, or about historical events, someone always manages to cry out for an alternative, and other voices chime in. I even looked up the word in the dictionary to make sure I understood it correctly. The brief definition was as follows: "Alternative—the need to choose between two or several phenomena that exclude one another." Will this "alternative thinking" of ours ultimately do us in? Is this why we still can't draw rational conclusions from the lessons of the past and adopt an acceptable programme to get us out of this terrible crisis? Is this why we want to turn away from all the experience of the past and once again fundamentally destroy everything we've had in order to build yet another new society? Is this why we are so quick to raise on a pedestal new idols and curse those who have not met our expectations? Some are willing to go so far as to dig people up out of their graves even though this is not worthy of civilized human beings. Can we be sure that suddenly some alternative won't be so triumphant that it will again claim monopoly of the truth?

No matter what anyone says, when I try to understand the intricacies of the past and the present, I prefer the outmoded method of materialist dialectics, which sees contradictions as the key to change, not alternatives. I see no other way to comprehend the complex and contradictory paths of our society, and to avoid these constant shifts from one extreme to the other, which we pay for at a very high price. If only politicians suffered from the consequences! More often than not millions of ordinary people pay most of the price.

This is why I have always avoided extremism, regardless of my personal likes and dislikes of major political leaders I have known in the recent past. That is why at the outset I want to disappoint anyone who expects me to divulge secret revelations about people who were once famous and influential but who are now considered odious figures whether or not the reputation is deserved.

I remember the smallest details of my meeting with Suslov. This is only understandable. I was still a young man and was going to have a complex conversation about the future of a major steel plant. The second man in the party made a deep and absolutely positive impression.

When I was led into his office, Suslov, a thin, tall, and slightly stooped man, came out from behind his desk and greeted me.

"Tell me, young man, show me where this Temirtau of yours is."

I went up to the big map of the Soviet Union that was hanging on the wall.

"Here it is, Mikhail Andreyevich. This is Kazakhstan, this is Karaganda, and nearby in the steppes, is the country's gigantic steel plant, a postwar strategic facility."

"Go on, go on."

I went on and told him everything as it was. I told him how the plant was built, how no thought was given to the people who worked there, about the hundreds of major defects in the construction, how anyone who wanted could take out truckloads of steel because there was no fence around it, about the shortage of housing, childcare centres, food, and necessary consumer goods, about the severe climate, the storms that kept people from getting to work, and about the women who had nowhere to work.

He listened to me very carefully; he never interrupted. Then he began asking questions, questions that showed he was interested in the smallest details. He made notes as I answered.

At the end of the conversation he asked: "What are you planning to tell the Secretariate tomorrow?"

I told him my presentation was ready.

"I advise you tomorrow to say everything you told me."

When I left his office I noticed that to the right of me, at the entrance, were a pair of galoshes. Something about them gave the room a feeling of home, something ordinary, although practically no one wore galoshes any more.

My conversation with Suslov made me more confident. First, I could expect that we would not be severely criticized. Second, it seemed that my account had touched him, that he was on our side and understood the problems we faced. After all, as I said, he listened very closely and asked questions about all the relevant matters of those days.

Young and inquisitive eyes can see a lot. I remember that before the hearing of our issue, right outside the doors to the room where the Secretariate was meeting, A. S. Kolebayev, Secretary of the Central Committee of the Kazakhstan Communist Party, went up to V. K. Akulintsev, Secretary of the Karaganda Regional Party Committee:

"Let me have a look at what you're going to say."

Akulintsev offered him the typed sheets of paper with his remarks. Kolebayev looked them over and said:

"Not bad. You know, I think this will be my presentation." With that, he put the paper in his suit pocket.

I don't know how Akulintsev felt at that moment, but I was absolutely shocked. However, that was not the end of the matter. After the plant's director and I spoke, Suslov asked who else wanted to say something. Akulintsev quickly went up to the platform with a copy of the same text that Kolebayev had taken from him, and without hesitating, he read it.

Strong criticism at the meeting was raised against the top officials of the ministry of metallurgy and heavy engineering. Suslov said, "You have turned a major government project into an organization of wheelers and dealers." The meeting ended with a decision to instruct the USSR Council of Ministers to adopt a resolution to improve the living conditions and recreational facilities of the steel workers of Kazakhstan. I was appointed to the commission that was to draw up this document. Naturally I'll never forget the figures that we put in the resolution. It was decided that annually we could expect 80,000 square meters of housing, two childcare centers for 1,660 children, and two vocational schools; we were also to build a new metallurgical vocational school, a new building for the main vocational school, a Palace of Culture, a sports complex, and a resort for the steel workers.

But as we know, even the best resolution passed at the highest level isn't necessarily implemented. Soon afterwards it turned out that it wasn't possible to build so many sites. This was one of those cases when it was a big help that the director and I worked so well together. He and I agreed on a way to get more construction workers. We decided to claim that the 1,500 employees we usually sent to help out on the farms during the harvest season continued to work there the rest of the time, but actually they were assigned to our construction projects.

The city began its transformation. Big apartment houses grew up, we gained eight new childcare centers, a stadium for 15,000, and a fifty meter swimming pool. On the right bank of the reservoir we built a resort and sanatorium. Our main accomplishment was to give housing to everyone on the waiting list. The turnover of workers at the plant immediately dropped from 32 to 9 or 10 per cent.

The results of our efforts proved to me that what's most important in any industry is the people. I realized that you couldn't do anything at all if you didn't create normal, dignified living and working conditions.

We found the resources to do away with the plant's shortfalls. In the course of that unpleasant, difficult, but necessary work, I was constantly amazed at the wasteful way in which the construction had been managed. The main problem was that the designs were absolutely useless. Millions of rubles were wasted on concrete, on foundations that were too big and yet inadequate. Later millions were spent on rectifying the mistakes. We also have to count the millions that were lost over the many years the plant could not produce at its planned capacity. This is just an example of one enterprise in one industry.

Gradually the plant began operating normally. By that time I began thinking about leaving my job with the party and going over to management where I felt I could be more directly involved with steel production. It's no secret that this was a realistic prospect for a party committee secretary in an industrial enterprise, and I liked the idea.

However, fate had something else in mind for me. Perhaps it would be more correct to say that it wasn't fate but people who had something different in mind for me. After all, one is dependent on people in this kind of party work. It was a reality of the times and had to be reckoned with.

Several years later, S. A. Kunayev, when he was in a good mood, told me that my presentation at the Secretariate of the Central Committee made a good impression, and note was taken of me. That is apparently one of the reasons why four years later I was recommended to be the secretary of the Karaganda Regional Party Committee in charge of industry.

The Karaganda Region is Kazakhstan's leading industrial area. At that time the annual output of industries in the region amounted to four billion rubles. The industries were coal, ferrous and non-ferrous metallurgy, chemical, petrochemical, and power. It was necessary to learn many things from scratch, and to re-analyze my work at a much higher level. My situation at this level was anything but simple. The director of the steel plant and I had worked well together, but our relations with our superiors were rather complex. We often had conflicts with the first secretary of the Temirtau City Party Committee and with the secretary of the regional committee. As a rule, they did not give us any significant support, but we could always count on them telling us what to do. Incidentally, when I talked about Dolgikh's visit to our plant in 1973 I didn't mention that this was the result of a memo I sent to the Central Committee about the catastrophic situation. It's common knowledge that the local leadership never encouraged such "initiative from below," and sometimes did not forgive it.

In my new job I had to make a serious choice about how I would live and act from then on. One way had been tried and tested for a long time by many representatives of more than one generation of party officials. This route necessitated strengthening one's position in the corridors of power, creating one's own impenetrable core in the complex hierarchical system, with its own laws concealed from outsiders. But during the years I worked at the steel plant I had learned another simple law—if you really want to work for people, then you have to rely on these people. I decided to stay with that rule.

I already had one strong support to rely on—the employees of the Karaganda Steel Plant, and its party organization that was then, and still is, Kazakhstan's biggest. Perhaps I overestimated what the steel workers thought of me, but I felt that if necessary they would support me. Apparently I had every reason to think so — for instance, last year, the steel workers voted for me in a secret ballot to be a delegate to the party congress. Although when I became secretary of the regional party committee it was not such a simple matter to appear at the plant in my new capacity. Sometimes my old friends at the blast furnace would criticize me:

"What are you doing with a white shirt on riding in a car? Have you forgotten who you were? Come on, get over to the blast furnace and see how we're working."

I would go there in my suit and tie even though the temperature was 70 degrees Celsius. After that I'd call together the party committee and give them three days to correct a problem, and I'd see to it myself that the job was done. If you don't keep your word to the steel workers you can't ever show your face there again. I would say the hardest part of the job was to win the trust of the miners. Miners accept only the people they accept. For them to accept you and talk straight to you, you have to go down into the shafts with them. They have no use for people who don't understand the character of a miner. In my opinion this is one of the main reasons for the conflicts that arose between the government and the miners in various coal regions of the country.

The Karaganda coal basin has twenty-six underground mines. I think that only the English mines are comparable in terms of the methane content, which is nineteen cubic meters per ton of coal. These mines are in constant danger of explosions and collapses because of the complex layers. I spent half a year visiting all the mines. I had various adventures at the mines. Once, a few meters away, a shaft collapsed, but no one was hurt. And there were situations when people were buried in rubble not so far away.

The Karaganda miners had a hard time; they did not reach planned targets. When I looked into the matter more thoroughly I realized that the problems in the coal basin were the same as the familiar problems of the steel plant, down to the last detail. Again, the trouble was with the centralized allocation of capital investments and the distribution of funds. Again the housing shortage was not within the scope of the government's interests. The former principle of "less spending and more output" kept new underground coal mines from being developed, and the city began, literally, to be undermined. The ground sank, water pipes broke, roads and buildings collapsed. However, no one could consider building new mines. This situation made the job of the miners harder and the chances of accidents greater. There was never enough of the necessary equipment, as if no one cared just how an increase in coal extraction was accomplished.

Once again it was imperative to complain to the central government. We wrote up a big report and sent it to the Central Committee of the CPSU, and to the national government. The result was that at the end of my first year as secretary of the regional party committee, the USSR Council of Ministers issued a resolution to improve the living conditions of the miners of Karaganda. We were able to build a huge number of apartments, considerably better community services, expand the thermal power plant, and make improvements on the mines.

Nevertheless, coal output at the old mines was still poor, and the workers were exhausted. Nikolai Drizhd, the general director of the coal mines, and I, began looking for a solution. We decided to put into operation an open cast mine called the Borlinsky. This offered some relief to the miners who were working underground, because it gave them time to develop new fields.

These situations, and the style of the centralized government, were common in both the seventies and eighties. In 1980, after I became a secretary of the Central Committee of the Communist Party of Kazakhstan, a cascade of electrical power plants was built on the Ekibastuz hydroelectric power station. I remember having to raise the traditional questions at the Central Committee in Moscow. Why was an electrical power plant being built but no repair system? Why weren't there regular deliveries of equipment? Why didn't the workers have adequate housing, recreation facilities, or childcare centres?

In general it was a vicious circle. Every breakthrough cost us tremendous efforts. It was increasingly clear that this vicious circle was caused by the hideously deformed economic system that had practically turned its back on the people's needs. In this respect Kazakhstan was a vivid example and could serve as a lesson to others.

The republic's wealth of resources provided the potential for strong mining, steel, energy, oil and chemical industries. In the first five-year-plan periods before World War II, the vast amounts of copper in Dzhezkazgan stimulated the development of our leading and unique non-ferrous metallurgy. The discovery of polymetals in central and eastern Kazakhstan prompted the development of the Soviet Union's largest enterprises supplying the country with one-third of its copper, seventy per cent of its zinc, over sixty per cent of its lead, and ninety per cent of its titanium and magnesium. The deposits of phosphorus in southern Kazakhstan, especially in Karatau, provide the country with ninety per cent of its yellow phosphorus output. The chrome deposits in the Aktyubinsk Region account for nearly all of the country's chrome, and ninety per cent of its export. Any schoolchild knows the economic importance of the Karaganda and Ekibastuz coal basins. In the 1980s, in western Kazakhstan, huge gas and oil fields began to be developed. In this context it should be stressed that Kazakhstan is also a major agricultural republic with forty million hectares of cultivated land. Grains are grown on twenty-five million hectares of this land, ten million heads of cattle are grazed there, along with forty million sheep and goats.

I think that even this brief account of the republic's economic role in the country is enough to compare it with just one paradoxical fact: sixty percent of Kazakhstan's consumer goods in those days had to be imported from other republics. Even this amount was insufficient to meet the people's needs. This was a vivid example of how all resources were put into the giants of heavy industry while the people's needs were put on hold. For decades the huge factory buildings, the cascades of electrical power plants, the powerful blast furnaces and enormous cranes were seen as the hope for a better future that became ever more transparent until it finally vanished into the stark reality of the present.

I must admit that I did not immediately understand that this kind of economy was leading us into a dead end. After all, the country had been developed like this for decades. It seemed eternal. It took a lot of time and experience to begin to question what seemed immutable. Naturally I did what I could to change what was obviously absurd. For instance, meat output was sufficient but there was no way to process it; there was a lot of milk but no way to process it; there was an enormous amount of rawhide but no tanneries. Our exports to other republics included a mere twelve to fifteen per cent of finished products; the rest were raw materials or semi-processed products.

The efforts of industrial directors and myself to convert heavy industry into light industry did not have tangible results. We needed huge investments to do this, but often we could not spend one ruble without permission from the central government. If we managed to get anything it was only due to our persistence. This is how we were able to remodel the fur plant in Semipalatinsk which had imported equipment and a planned capacity of 30,000 sheepskin coats a year.

Time showed that the distorted economic integration within the country threatened to have dangerous political consequences. This became clearer when the republics began gaining sovereign rights. Now people realize that the republics with natural resources are being subsidized. How could it be otherwise when the prices of raw materials are so deformed that they bear no relation to their real value in terms of the labour that goes into their output? I can give many painful examples. The extraction and enrichment of alumina account for eighty per cent of the labour that goes into the final product of aluminium. Although the factories that actually produce the aluminium from the raw material contribute five per cent of the labour, they receive eighty per cent of the profit. Meanwhile Kazakhstan suffers all the environmental hazards of the extraction and enrichment. The situation is similar with Dzhezkazgan and Balkhash copper, which is sent to other republics in its raw form. We are not trusted with the production of gold and silver bars; all we can do is export the silver and gold alloys to other regions, even though it wouldn't be difficult for us to process them. Incidentally, over half the country's silver comes from Kazakhstan. To me and to any sensible economist it is absolutely clear that republics with raw materials should not be subsidized, but that the money we have lost unfairly should be returned. I also don't believe that the republics should present their grievances based on the archaic pricing system resulting from the fifties.

Looking back on those difficult times when we spent all our energy on boosting our economic machine, on keeping it from falling apart, I think a lot about the charge some make that we were only prolonging the agony, postponing the inevitable collapse. I don't think we were. The country was alive and working hard. Contrary to common thinking, the "period of stagnation" had many facets. For some reason many people say that during this period the top leadership spent all its time boasting to the public but creating havoc behind the scenes, while the ordinary population was reeling. I believe that this kind of thinking is excusable only if it is based on knowledge from newspaper articles and not on personal experience.

I never cease to be amazed by the natural wisdom and insight of working people. If anyone, let's say in 1980, went to a factory party meeting and tried to say something nice about Brezhnev, "the outstanding political leader and statesman," the workers would look at that person strangely. However people always reacted with understanding and a sense of responsibility to serious suggestions and important undertakings. Today they talk a lot about the former numerous absurd "initiatives." But the only people who were extremely enthusiastic about them were the pencil-pushing bureaucrats who were afraid to show their faces around the workers in an ordinary factory setting. I remember many examples of other, more admirable types of behaviour.

While I was still working at the Karaganda Steel Plant, in the most difficult years when planned targets were not being reached, rank and file communists, ordinary workers, initiated some wonderful patriotic practices. For instance, a work team headed by a communist named Sabelnikov decided that if one of them violated labour discipline, all of them would take the blame and lose all their bonuses. Wasn't this a step toward the future idea of contract teams who take full responsibility for the end product, and whose pay depends entirely on the results of their labour? Just try and think up such a plan in a district party committee and suggest it to the workers. You'll get nowhere.

I think the seeds of the ideas for our current reforms evolved among the workers and particularly the new members. This is where the understanding grew that we could not go on like that anymore. In our haste to throw out everything we inherited from the "period of stagnation" we are losing an important instrument of radical reform of the economy and the whole society—the very discipline that the party was able to ensure. On many occasions, as I have already said, in the most difficult and critical moments, it was possible to mobilize party members to restore order in the shops, to prevent anarchy, and stop slipshod habits. All management structures were subject to party discipline. To be sure, many things were done wrong. In order to ensure that managers be accountable, they had to be party members. As a result, the country lost many talented experts and organizers. Managers were always in jeopardy of party reprimands. It was possible in a year to receive a dozen or so strong reprimands through administrative channels, but just one reprimand from the city or the district party committee was enough to upset a person's life for years to come.

Party discipline was the framework of power. We have destroyed this framework, but unfortunately have not been able to replace it with anything new. Furthermore, we have created chaos all the way through the system, from top to bottom. When we say we have no strategy for perestroika, what I think is that the Soviets to whom we tried to transfer the party's power were not ready for it. After all, they traditionally did not play a role as initiators; they were just supposed to follow orders and carry out resolutions and directives.

In anticipation of strong objections to my opinion I would like to stress that I am not among those who long for a strong leader. It could also be pointed out that necessary discipline is one thing, but dictates by the party are quite another and totally unacceptable. However I wouldn't put into one category party leadership, even with all its past shortcomings, and the dictates of the administrative—command system. Recent developments show that these are not one and the same thing. Only pathological hatred of communists could keep one from seeing that the party bodies that have transferred power to the Soviets no longer have any real power. At the same time, national agencies and ministries still have a tight grip on distribution in the economy, and are the vehicles of the administrative-command system. True, it is no longer necessary to follow their orders down to every detail, and there are no longer the same economic levers that punished disobedience. Hence the decline of the customary system of connections. Apparently neither the party nor its apparatus that had taken on the whole burden of political and economic leadership noticed that they were serving as a prop for the administrative bodies that remained behind the scenes.

I am convinced that if we don't restore discipline to the economy, we will inevitably slide to the bottom of the abyss. Nothing will save us, not the market or privatization because a self-governing economy without a government or discipline is only a myth. I don't want to go into the experiences of other countries because everyone tends to talk about only what they like. But I want to mention one general consistency—the countries that firmly took the route of a market economy in the postwar period started by ensuring strict discipline in the economic and other spheres. Examples of this are South Korea, Taiwan and Turkey.

I certainly don't want to justify the methods of party leadership that discredited themselves to the people forever. The country was seriously harmed when unlimited power was concentrated among a few people. Recently much justified criticism has been leveled against Leonid Brezhnev and his team. Still I would not be in a hurry to condemn all of Brezhnev's associates, especially those who are now deceased. If some day we really begin to understand our past, we can probably understand the people who lived and worked in those days. It is no wonder we say that to understand is to forgive. For many years the history of Kazakhstan was linked with Dinmukhamed Kunayev, one of Brezhnev's closest associates. They had many bonds. In the Virgin Lands Brezhnev devoted several pages to Kunayev and highly valued their twenty-year friendship. Everyone in Kazakhstan knew about that and it lent great prestige to the republic's leader. The First Secretary of the Central Committee of the Kazakhstan Communist Party handled all the republic's affairs. Every single official, in the party and in the government, as well as all state farm directors, were appointed with his approval. Kunayev regarded the Kazakhstan Council of Ministers as one big Central Committee department.

My first close acquaintance with Brezhnev was in 1980. Kazakhstan was celebrating its sixtieth anniversary together with all the Politburo members of the national Central Committee. The impression Brezhnev made was terrible. He had no expression in his eyes and walked with great difficulty. He had to be supported on both sides by two hefty men.

I remember two episodes. During a break in the meeting, the whole leadership gathered in a room to the side of the stage. It was very hot and humid, so we drank tea and took off our jackets. Brezhnev was suddenly called to the phone. When he returned (he was brought back by the same two men), he shared the news in a loud voice: "Gierek insists on a meeting. But Andropov's people say we shouldn't agree under any circumstances. He seems to be a goner now. They say there's a good fellow there—Kania."

Events in Poland were complex at that time, but I was able to evaluate that conversation when Kania became the leader of the Polish party. That is how matters were decided that affected the lives of millions of people.

Another incident took place during a huge reception held in the foyer of the Auezov Theater. There were around a thousand guests. Tables were placed on two levels. Everyone had just sat down when Kunayev made a toast to Leonid Brezhnev, to the marshal of the party, the marshal of the army, etc. Just as soon as people took a sip and put down their glasses, the main guest of honor suddenly stood up and headed toward the exit. Naturally everyone in the leadership followed him. Brezhnev went outside, got into his car, and a minute later the whole cortege drove away. It was quite clear that he had simply forgotten where he was and why he had come. What can you feel for such a person other than pity?

When I was approved to join the Secretariat of the Kazakhstan Central Committee, Suslov recalled our conversation about the problems at the Karaganda Steel Plant (or perhaps someone reminded him) and commented, "So we developed you." It's true that my new job depended on the opinion of one of the top party leaders and on the approval of Kunayev who needed people who had practical experience in the republic's industry. However I think that up to that point in my life I can say that my development was really due to other people.

Despite the "stagnation" our people were capable of conscious discipline, sincere enthusiasm, and creativity. You have a strong confirmation of this. Do you think it is possible to nurture these qualities today in this critical period before new economic levers are functioning?

Unquestionably, enthusiasm was evident even in the stagnant years. But it was not the kind of enthusiasm we saw in the preceding decades. First, it was not a unanimous, collective response to general mottos and appeals. Second, many initiatives arose despite the traditional economic policies, the outmoded methods of management and industrial organization. I cited the example of how a prototype of a contract team was developed. But this creative, sincere enthusiasm, and seeds of the new ways could not grow outside the framework of the tightly regulated economic system. People joked that any initiative was subject to punishment, but this was tragically the case for many enterprising managers. We know many examples of people who actually went to jail for their creative efforts.

My direct and brief answer to your question is that we can't hope to motivate the people to follow us by using high-sounding words. For too long we exploited the enthusiasm of our trusting and responsive people. Before World War II, especially during the period of industrialization, people accepted the socialist slogans and believed that they could make a better life for themselves by working hard. It is also understandable that the people were so self-sacrificing during the postwar reconstruction when the country was in ruins. A little later people were promised communism in the near future. All they had to do was work a bit harder. But that bright future never came. Then we heard another slogan—that we were living for future generations. I think this simply goes against human nature. No-one in the world but us could ever get such an absurd idea. Again I recall how young people from the west at the World Youth Festival were so surprised and critical when we tried to explain the substance of this ideal.

The role of socialist emulation became meaningless along with the dashed hopes that people had for a better future. Although the idea was basically good, it could not function anymore based only on moral motivation. I remember that A. N. Kosygin's principle was that if there is a shortage of fuel, it's necessary to give bonuses for every ton of coal or oil extracted. However, this was only good for short-term success. The workers did not have a constant motivation for better work.

Everywhere in the world there is emulation, only it is tough and it is called by its real name, competition. In our transition to a market economy in Kazakhstan we began by drafting anti-monopoly legislation and establishing an Anti-Monopoly Commission. These measures are intended to promote competition between manufacturers that should boost productivity and quality. Such competition should provide equal conditions for various forms of ownership, and do away with political levers in the economy. Perhaps to us this system seems rather harsh, but without such motivation that has worked throughout the world, we will not have any breakthrough in our economy.

You touched on the problem of motivation in the old economic system. But you also said that essentially our people have lost their ideals, their hope in the future. There are two points of view on this. Some believe that the party leadership and the administrative-command system compromised the socialist idea and others insist that the idea itself is flawed. What is your opinion?

The point is that we simply do not know any other socialism than the one that our fathers and ourselves experienced. We learned this idea from childhood at school, and believed it was the only true and humane idea. We never had a chance to look at it from a different angle. Now we all have that possibility, so we have to try to calmly and objectively appraise our past and compare it to the nature and trends of world development.

We always had different interpretations of socialist ideas that are fundamentally in the best interests of humanity. For instance, look at the history of the international communist movement and the splits within that movement. At the same time, there are a number of developed capitalist countries where socialists have headed the government, or are at the helm today, and successfully manage the economy with a developed market structure that, in the opinion of many of our social scientists, has nothing to do with classical socialism.

It's wrong to ignore the importance and consequences of the 1917 socialist revolution. It undoubtedly had an enormous impact on the capitalist world, primarily by compelling capitalism to look after the interests of the workers and to move toward democratizing social relations. But our revolutionaries interpreted Marxism dogmatically. They regarded the revolution as an immediate transition to the commune and did everything to make this happen, totally disregarding the circumstances. As we know the theoreticians justified this experiment. This led to a totalitarian regime in which the people were thought of as "human material," to use Nikolai Bukharin's expression. We were constantly told that everything should be done for the sake of people, but in actuality the goal of our revolution was not the human being, but socialism understood in the abstract. Who needs the kind of socialism in which people have less value than a sack of cement? This is not a metaphor. We need only to recall how the great construction projects of the twenties and thirties were accomplished. I don't want to argue about what real socialism is. Let's leave that to the social scientists. To me it is absolutely clear that we can't go on living the way we did. If anyone wants to call what we saw socialism, that's fine with me. But it is simply immoral to try and prove that it was the best system. If it was the best, then it's not at all clear why we are so far behind the countries that we beat in the war, even though we started postwar construction basically as equals. I can draw only one conclusion — on the international scene our system could not compete.

If I'm asked directly whether I support the socialist choice I say yes without hesitation. But what I support is not some dogma, but my own understanding of socialism. We always learned in school that socialism is a society in which the guiding principle is "From each according to his abilities, to each according to his work." I have to agree with that. But what was the reality? We were constantly suppressing capability and creative talent, and instead of paying people what they deserved, we paid them all the same, no matter how they performed. So what we have to do is make this principle a reality.

You talked about the work of the miners. Now it is one of the country's biggest problems. Do you see a way to solve this major conflict, and particularly in the Karaganda coal basin?

I think that I not only mentioned the Karaganda miners, but have generally answered this question. The reasons for the conflict lie in the "vicious circle" that I talked about and that we are still trying to unwind with great difficulty. We have to talk not only about the miners, but also about the whole situation with the working class, the main producers of our material wealth. Throughout the civilized world the economy is intended to satisfy the people's needs, but in this country people are born to serve the interests of the economy which long ago became a self-reproducing system. This is simply absurd when we spend only thirty per cent of our national revenues on people, and the rest continues to go into building the foundations of new construction sites or on the defense industry.

This policy has had a particularly bad effect on the miners. Their work is especially hard and dangerous and so they require different living and social conditions. I think that in order to ease tensions in this industry it is necessary to put the miners in control of the coal they extract, or at least give them ten per cent of the coal to do with as they please. I don't understand why the national government still can't make this step. Of course, this won't solve the whole problem, but it will help them use the profits to buy food, consumer goods and satisfy other important needs. This is, of course, not the best way to spend hard currency. But we have no other choice right now. This is the only way to resolve the crisis.

However, the problem in general has to be solved in more fundamental ways. Today, for instance, the miners are criticized for the fact that all the mines are subsidized. By keeping the industry subsidized, the state keeps it under its control. This is due to the deformations in pricing. On the world market Karaganda coal costs thirty dollars a ton. Our own state has set the price at six and a half rubles on the domestic market. You can see the big difference. That's why I wouldn't be so fast in blaming the miners. I truly regret that many of the miners blindly followed the politicians in this complex situation, and made unconstitutional political demands that heightened tensions to the limit. I know very well that miners are a disciplined people. They appreciate order and therefore should realize the consequences of ignoring the law, the nation's Constitution.

CHAPTER FIVE

How Problems Were Solved

No matter what anyone says, no one so far has given a definitive answer to the main question concerning our country's future. No one has said how we can lead the country out of the economic crisis, the deepening political crisis, the crisis of ethnic relations, and a whole number of other difficult social problems. Of course we can construct various models of our new common home and the principles for managing the economy. We can even assume and agree that these models are viable. After all, we are often offered recipes that, as a rule, are tried and tested and have worked well in other countries. But it seems much harder to understand ourselves and explain to others how we can get into this new home without running into unforeseen obstacles that will upset what remains of our stability and strength.

I think that many troubles we have already experienced and are continuing to experience are due to our vague understanding of what we have, what we need to take with us, and what we need to discard. Unfortunately, we find people who think we either have to take everything or discard everything. It is no wonder that the hottest argument has been between the advocates of a so-called planned socialist economy and its opponents. It's a shame that so much energy is spent on these disputes instead of on our society's vast problems. As a matter of fact, I strongly believe that this is a useless debate. I don't believe that in the past three decades we have really had a planned economy. All we had were terms invented by obliging social scientists and economists. What we had were other methods of management that were disorganized and irresponsible, and came from the administrative–command system. One of our biggest problems that we inherited from the past was the social sciences that served the doctrines of the top leadership. And so now we are totally helpless to develop any viable theory. How many pseudo-scientific treatises were written just about one comment that Brezhnev made in public, that the economy should be economic. Everyone also remembers the "theory" of developed socialism, the "law-governed and lengthy stage of social progress." It would take too much time to enumerate all these ideas. So let's leave our "theoreticians" alone now and see what our system looked like in reality.

The main instrument we had for resolving major economic problems was invented back in 1867 by the Scotsman Alexander Bell—the telephone. I can give the example of how the Semipalatinsk fur coat plant was remodelled. I had a meeting with Gorbachev about this when he was at the Politburo and in charge of agriculture and light industry. I told him that we could make very good sheepskin coats out of our local raw materials. He called the Minister of Light Industry, a man named Tarasov, and within half a year we had imported equipment for that plant.

Such strategically important problems as the distribution of labour were resolved in the most arbitrary ways. Instead of building some small consumer goods plants in areas with surplus labour, we would erect gigantic plants employing 10,000 to 15,000 workers. For instance, under the pretext of employing the women of Kustanai, a huge textile plant was built. When the women were placed in their jobs it turned out that there weren't enough jobs for men. I found out accidentally that somewhere in Yelabuga there were plans to build a diesel engine plant. I figured it would be good to have that plant in Kustanai. That would take care of the serious economic and demographic problems.

I went to Moscow and called on A. P. Kirilenko. He certainly made me feel welcome, even kissed me for some reason, and offered me a chair. I spent a long time telling him about our plans, and I think I was very convincing. I saw that he wasn't listening attentively, just letting everything go in one ear and out the other. At the end of this strange conversation he asked me:

"So what is your problem?"

"I would like the diesel engine plant to be built in Kazakhstan."

He immediately called in a department head at the Central Committee, a man named Frolov, called the Minister of the Auto Industry, Polyakov, and resolved the problem within a matter of ten minutes.

That is how all serious economic matters were resolved.

I was especially amazed when I became the Chairman of the Kazakhstan Council of Ministers. I just started the job when the chairman of the republic's State Planning Committee came to me and requested bonuses for all his assistants and department heads, bonuses as big as their monthly salaries.

"What have they done to earn these bonuses?" I asked in amazement.

"Don't you know that we're going to Moscow to defend the plan for next year?"

"So what?"

"Well, we'll have to work with all the department heads at the State Planning Committee, invite them to our rooms and offer them hospitality."

Two days later the minister of finance came to my office:

"We're going to Moscow to defend the budget. Please give bonuses to me and my assistants."

Such practices were essentially open policy. I happened to be in Moscow when the republics' plans were being defended at the State Planning Committee. On the first floor of the building there were generous helpings of traditional food and dances organized from whatever republic happened to be defending its plan. So these officials not only had drinking parties.

This became such a usual practice that there was a time when the State Planning Committee wouldn't allow anyone into the building with bags. But people adapted to this restriction rather quickly. People would leave their presents down at the entrance in cloakroom shelves and call the person it was meant for to come and pick it up. I'll never forget how my predecessors told me in all seriousness how one national minister liked piglets, and how another liked receiving fresh tomatoes.

You can imagine what this "scientific" approach to devising plans and budgets was worth—if piglets and chateau wines were fundamental to this work. It was apparently hard for the chairman of our State Planning Committee and the minister of finance to defend the republic's plan and budget for 1985, because I never gave them those bonuses.

I'd like to give a general picture of this simple, almost primitive system on which our economy was based. Everything, to the last kopeck of the profits that came from enterprises, regions and republics, was sent to Moscow. Then Moscow divided up the budget, funds and resources. If you were on good terms with the minister of finance you could get a few million extra rubles. If you were friends with the chairman of the State Supplies Committee you could have cement, metal, and timber. No one particularly cared that they were taking someone else's share out of the common pot, nor suffered any guilty conscience. It was all you could do sometimes to fill in your own gaps.

The prevalence of this centralized administrative-command system corrupted management. Whether you liked it or not you had to follow the unwritten laws, so you had to fawn, give presents,and offer hospitality. Otherwise not you but your republic, your industry, your factory would have to go on a starvation diet. The only way to get money was to be clever and resourceful. This was the wellspring of the degradation, bribery, and corruption. The system forced so many people into crime.

As chairman of the republic's Council of Ministers I saw over and over how the USSR State Planning Committee and the USSR State Supplies Committee made it look on paper as if the plan was being carried out. Plans were approved even when everyone knew quite well that we had only seventy to eighty per cent of the resources, when everyone realized that the whole effort would inevitably fail. Hence the imbalance throughout the country, hence our troubles, our planned troubles.

Incidentally, even if planned targets were not met locally, even if they were far from reached, all was not lost. People had contacts, so they would appeal to the ministries, to the Council of Ministers, to the State Committee on Statistics, and to the Central Committee in order to revise the planned targets. This was also an important way to get positive indicators. For instance, the coal basin was not meeting its deadlines. First the deadlines would be changed from the first to the second quarter of the year, then from the second to the third, and from the third to the fourth. As a result, in December when calculations showed that the area had fallen short of its planned targets by several million rubles it was clear that people would not take first place in socialist emulation, and would lose their bonuses. This was when the most disgusting activities began, when it was necessary to persuade the minister to cancel the plan. Naturally this was done at the expense of the successful enterprises. These problems, like many others, could also be resolved sometimes by picking up the phone five minutes before the New Year, on December 31, when it was possible, with the help of the Central Committee department overseeing your industry and your minister, finally to convince the chairman of the State Committee on Statistics.

Chaos in the planning system was made worse by the fact that rubles were the only way we evaluated whether targets were reached. Actual output was not taken into account, although in their public speeches officials would boast of millions or billions of tons, square meters, or kilowatt hours of the output of one product or another. This approach to keeping track of the most important economic indicators—the gross national product, labour productivity, etc.— was absurd not only because of the primitve, unscientific system of price formation. This approach essentially had us counting our rubles repeatedly, which was grand and deliberate self-deception. For instance, let's say the Pavlodar Tractor Plant produces a tractor worth 4,000 rubles and sells it to an enterprise that manufactures bulldozers by simplying installing the blade. This plant adds to the 4,000 the 1,000 that the blade costs, and sells the piece of machinery for 5,000 rubles. This process can be repeated many times over in industry.

Furthermore, the cost of the raw materials, the semi-finished materials and parts that has already been included in the price is invariably repeated in the estimates as the manufacturing cycle continues, not only from year to year, but sometimes from five-year plan to five-year plan. As a result we have absolutely no idea about our real gross national product. According to the experts, our real GNP in the recent past was barely half of what we presented in our official statistics. This "Scientific" approach to solving fundamental problems in our economy led to a paradoxical phenomenon. It made more sense for an enterprise to operate according to the principle "the worse the better." The worse you worked, the more you received, because if you increased the materials that went into your product its price soared. Why make miniature switches for machinery when the revenues were hundreds of times more for producing enormous outmoded switches? Why use inexpensive but sturdy materials in construction when the assembly of huge and expensive concrete blocks and panels would easily ensure reaching the biggest targets estimated in rubles?

I still can't understand why our whole country engaged in this deception. Actually this approach in industry and other branches of the economy is still used today. It is especially disastrous now when inflation is so great. I think we have completely lost all sense of reality, and don't understand what is going on in the economy.

When I say that we should not condemn every former party and government official without question I am thinking of the many honest and talented people who because of the times were simply forced to cope within the strict framework of the administrative-command system. And that system often mercilessly threw overboard whoever was unnecessary. You could cry all you want to your wife about how unfairly you were treated, how you were fighting for a good cause; you could even publish in some dissident underground press. It would not affect anyone in the least.

I will never believe those who boast of being courageous champions of the truth but who, in the recent past, after running into some trouble, crawled into a hole and poured out their grief to friends in the safe refuge of their homes. This is not even to mention people with the amazing ability to change colours immediately when the wind blows in another direction.

In the most difficult of circumstances the vast majority of honest people continued to work no matter what. Furthermore, in local party and governing bodies they carried a double burden. For instance, a department official in the national Central Committee overseeing affairs in your republic could develop any opinion about you. All anonymous complaints were thoroughly investigated, and it was not at all hard to write them. Even if the "information didn't coincide with the facts," any written complaint against you was put in your file just in case something else might come up, on the assumption that there was no smoke without fire. The head of the Central Committee department in charge of your region was like a tsar, a God. Everything depended on the written document he would issue and send to his superiors. This document sealed your fate, so you were better off to acquiesce. The people who were higher up were even stronger. They could decide the fate of anybody in one hour. At any local party plenum or bureau meeting the vote would be in favour of a recommendation made from above or the person would "ask" to be transferred to another job.

I don't think that anyone felt pressure from totalitarianism as much as local leaders. Hardly anything outside the framework of official opinion could be mentioned out loud. Even as Secretary of the Central Committee of the Kazakhastan Communist Party I had no insurance against the all-seeing eyes of those above me. The first secretary of the republic knew absolutely everything about what you did even after working hours. He knew who invited you over for dinner, who you took walks with at the vacation resort, who you talked with and the subject of your conversations. A small group of close associates of the first secretary did virtually all the work. We secretaries of the Central Committee who were members of the bureau of the republic's Central Committee often heard about personnel appointments, transfers and other important matters only after the fact. A person who was received in Kunayev's house could decide the fate of someone else by issuing promotions, dismissals, rewards, or apartments.

As chairman of the Council of Ministers I decided to look into the affairs of the republic's Academy of Sciences. We had known for a long time that there was no real leadership in the Academy, that no serious academic research was under way, and that it was only functioning to issue postgraduate degrees to relatives of academicians and, naturally, of the president of the academy, Askar Kunayev. The latter was a younger brother of the first secretary. Everyone knew that the president was an alcoholic, that he went in search of drinking partners every night to the homes of his employees, and staggered into all sorts of dubious places. It was a rare day when he came to work sober, nevertheless he was influential since he was the one who decided whether someone was made an academician or a corresponding member of the Academy, was appointed rector of any institution of higher learning, or given a higher degree. Realizing that this could not go on any longer I went to have a frank talk with Dinmukhamed

Kunayev about putting a rein on his brother, since no one else had any influence on him. It seemed that Dinmukhamed Akhmedovich took to heart what I said, but a day later Askar called me in his usual state asking why I disliked him. The whole conversation was a classical example of how drunks talk outside a liquor store when one party is trying to explain something while the other one constantly interrupts with the question, "Hey, don't you respect me?"

It took considerable energy to keep from getting entangled in the harsh nets of party-administrative dictates, to stay out of the trap of nepotism. This unjust system went against the grain of any decent person. Inevitably most people were not only indignant but wanted to resist this entrenched system.

I believe that it was in the mid-seventies that understanding of the need for changes developed in party organizations, in various leadership bodies of the party from the bottom up. That was when it became obvious that party activities were increasingly formalistic and made to look more effective by false statistics. Secretaries of party organizations were forced to exaggerate in their reports the number of communists who attended general meetings, and prepare heaps of unnecessary paperwork. Work with human beings was secondary. The main thing for party organizers was to write up glowing reports and turn them in on time. Their work was evaluated in the district party committees by how it looked on paper. The more these administrative methods of managing party organizations took hold, the less vitality there was in all the party's activities.

There were people who adapted to this quickly. Careerists flocked into the party. This change turned the workers away from the party. It became necessary to maintain working class membership artificially, which couldn't help but affect the kind of people we had involved. The party began to degenerate. This is the main reason why the party so rapidly relinquished many of its positions in the ensuing political struggle when the healthy core of the Communist party decisively took the course of radical reforms. Obviously, in order to get off to a running start it had to begin perestroika by making changes in its own ranks.

The main indicator for Kazakhstan was the amount of grain it sold the state. This is where all of its efforts were focused. A journalistic cliche, "the battle for bread," can be frequently seen in the newspapers during the harvest season. The farmers really have to work hard, mobilize their courage and patience.

Nevertheless it doesn't seem quite right to compare farm work with a battle, because there is nothing more peaceable than this kind of labour. I think it makes more sense to compare the situation at various levels of power during this period with warfare. Moreover, the battle is not so much for bread, but for titles and awards.

Every year these "bread battles" were waged about the same time, in early August. If it looked like the harvest would be good, the General Secretary of the party was immediately informed and invited to visit the republic. No matter what happened, everyone was supposed to know and understand that the amount of wheat to be brought in and sold was already calculated, and had to be delivered at all costs. So tremendous pressure was put to bear on regional leaders. Very few of them put up any resistance since they knew that in the fall a shower of medals would descend, and with them, perhaps a gold Hero of Socialist Labour medal. By that time it wouldn't matter whether the region reached its targets in industry, building, or agriculture. The first secretary of the regional party committee could be awarded the title of Hero of Socialist Labour after reaching the planned target for grain only once in five years, even if no targets for the whole five-year period were accomplished. It was a simple matter because everything depended on what the first secretary of the republic decided, since the central leadership left it all up to him. I think that all the people who received those medals realized this. This is perhaps the reason why these days they don't ever wear the medals.

This is the way many party officials and managers received their awards. I can't say that none of them deserved any medals. As a rule, most of them worked hard and selflessly. However the criteria for evaluating their work were distorted. I would especially like to stress that no one has any reason to question the medals that ordinary workers received. The farm workers, the coal miners, the steel workers earned their awards with their own sweat, often undermining their health and suffering deprivations. These people are not to blame that politics were played at their expense. During the "battle for bread" no one gave any thought to the fact that Kazakhstan was in a high risk agricultural zone. The only way to ensure that the republic kept its word to the central government was for party officials from Moscow to visit the local areas constantly and do whatever they thought necessary—make threats, reprimands, wine and dine, appeal to conscience and responsibility to the party. It was believed that any means used were justified because the country needed wheat. Those who, after a really serious inspection of the farms doubted the harvest prospects, were taken off the job beforehand. This was done to prevent disorganization among the people and to set an example.

As a result of this approach, Kazakhstan was unable to increase its meat output in the eleventh five-year-plan period. The state-owned and collective farms had to completely empty their own granaries in order to reach the targets set by the state, and then buy concentrated fodder for their livestock at triple the price. But the directors and chairmen of these farms knew that if they didn't have fodder the state would give them subsidies, and if necessary, they would ask for the same wheat back from the government. These were typical methods for solving economic problems under the administrative-command system.

The more I learned about agricultural management, the more I realized that Kazakhstan's leaders were getting honours for essentially fictitious accomplishments. I spent a lot of time talking to agricultural experts at the USSR Academy of Agriculture, specialists at the institute of grain cultivation in the Tselinograd Region, directors of state-owned farms, managers, and agronomists in order to understand the real situation. I was convinced that these people truly cared about agriculture, and did everything they could to help correct the problems. I began with the most basic task, to determine the republic's real agricultural potential. The first step was to combat the practice of falsely declaring output figures.

For instance, when Sagidulla Kubashev was appointed first secretary of the Semipalatinsk regional party committee, he found out that his area had actually 330,000 heads of livestock less than was reported. He told me this "great" news when I visited Semipalatinsk.

"What are you planning to do?" I asked Kubashev.

"What can I do? I fired several managers, some now face criminal charges. But up there," he paused, then pointed his finger up in the air, "they told me not to make much noise and offered to restore the right number of livestock within a year."

He had no choice but to agree. They got all the livestock without any fanfare.

These were not the only such examples. That's why I sent official letters twice in 1985 to the bureau of the Kazakhstan party Central Committee asking permission to recount all the livestock in the republic. Both times the answer was a categorical no. I had to begin this work illegally — literally. I was helped by Boris Isayev, the chair of the republic's Committee of People's Control, an honest and uncompromising man. We involved in our efforts the office of the Council of Ministers, People's Control, trade unions, and individuals at the Ministry of Finance. We uncovered many interesting but unfortunate facts. For instance, there was supposed to be a big herd of horses near Kzyl-Orda, with one herder and an assistant. It turned out that the herder and his assistant really did exist, at least they regularly signed for their pay. But there was no herd. We found that it was typical for a herd to contain both state-owned and personal livestock. It was possible for a herder to turn in his "own" livestock for 30,000 to 50,000 rubles. Local meat packers paid out this money without asking any questions. Many local officials also had no qualms about feeding their own livestock at the government's expense.

As the head of government I began receiving information that aides of the first secretary of the Kazakhstan party were abusing their powers for self-serving purposes by influencing promotions, the distribution of housing and awards. All this was done with Kunayev's protection. Either that or people would slip him such resolutions to sign. I had a frank talk with him, but I didn't get any further than I had when we talked about the president of the republic's Academy of Sciences.

The longer this went on the worse it got. Apparently the extent of the powers of our top officials was so great that they decided to build pompous structures. With unprecedented energy they built not only administrative buildings but even a city bathhouse. Clearly there weren't enough centralized funds for all this, so money was taken out of the funds intended for rural construction and from the municipal budget. As a result there was much less money allocated for other needs in Alma-Ata — roads, housing, and other municipal facilities.

All my attempts to raise these issues were met with profound but concealed irritation. Finally I was told that everything in Kazakhstan was just fine and I shouldn't clean dirty laundry in public. Nor was there any useful response to my detailed report on the serious problems with livestock breeding. At that time, May 15, 1985, just before a regular full-scale meeting of the republic's Central Committee, I asked for permission to address the regional party and government officials. I was allotted forty minutes. In that time I tried to analyze the serious negative phenomena that had developed in Alma-Ata and in most of the regions. After my presentation there was dead silence in the hall. When I left the podium Kunayev, who was chairing the meeting, made the final comments:

"The information will be taken into account. The meeting is adjourned."

A wall of alienation rose between Kunayev's associates and myself.

Based on what you say, we can conclude that because of the incompetence of our experts, even debates about critical economic issues are still rather dogmatic in nature. Judging by a number of your publications, you are anything but an amateur when it comes to these questions. This is also evident from your dissertation in economics that was approved last year. Why did you decide to do this academic work? Is this part of the trend of top leaders thinking they have to have a higher degree? Are you planning to continue with your academic work?

I became seriously interested in economics when I was still in college. It grew out of my experience at the Karaganda Steel Plant and my rather sad observations of how the industry functions. I noticed that in processing the ores many valuable components were wasted. I dealt with this in my graduation thesis at college. I have always been interested in this problem, as you can see from my dissertation, which is a study of conserving resources. I used the data that I collected over the years. After all, as a party official I was always dealing with economic issues, in Temirtau, Karaganda, and in the republic's Central Committee. This means that a party official is not so much involved in political matters as in economic affairs. It was necessary to delve into literally all aspects of the economy and industry. Party and economic management work were so intertwined that party bodies often functioned more like suppliers, especially during crisis situations. And while I was chair of the republic's Council of Ministers for over five years my work was focused on the economy. Incidentally, party leaders were not supposed to do academic work or write dissertations because it was felt that their positions put pressure on scholars and academic institutions to approve their work whether or not it was worthy.

However, in the seventies, when I was secretary of the party committee at the Karaganda plant and studied at the Higher Party School in the CPSU Central Committee, my teachers and advisors of my graduation thesis convinced me that I had to continue working on this subject no matter what because it was of great practical value. After all, Kazakhstan, as I have already said, is rich in natural resources. But because of our traditional approach to extracting this wealth we have already wasted sixteen billion tons of various mineral resources. For instance, the Sokolovsko-Sarbaisky plant annually dumps millions of tons of iron, thousands of tons of cobalt, vanadium, and nickel. No other place in the world is so wasteful with its precious raw materials. Recycling resources is invaluable, but this is something that we haven't even begun. Our increases in output were only in monetary terms. Enterprises did everything to inflate their output in this way. They didn't have the time, the resources or the technology to find ways to recycle all the valuable components of industrial work. But this would be much easier and cheaper than extracting more and more resources from the earth.

The problem of recycling is not only relevant to mineral resources. For instance, the oil deposits of western Kazakhstan contain enormous amounts of gas, in addition to sulphur. Around these areas it's possible to introduce the production of polymers, which would be profitable not only to the republic, but also to the whole country.

We do not have a comprehensive system for processing agricultural products, so we are losing much of what we grow and thus do not exploit our potential for increased output. For instance, if we made better use of waste products from the milling industry we could have much greater output of meat.

I could cite numerous examples since I know this subject very well and am extremely concerned about the problem. It is especially timely and significant now when we are trying to change to a market economy. Together with major western companies we are creating joint ventures for processing raw materials. We are also promoting the conversion of our defense industry, especially middle engineering. Besides, it's long overdue for us to stop thinking that our natural resources are inexhaustible. These resources cannot be restored. We have to think seriously about the future. As for my own plans for continuing to study the problem of resource conservation, they depend on how much time I have, which is never enough. I'm not interested in publishing academic papers, but in keeping up with advanced thinking about the economy.

You just talked about working with western companies, primarily involved in developing natural resources. By bringing western business into this fundamental industry don't you risk "selling the republic," as some people have charged?

Yes, I have heard this complaint, that we are selling away our resources as a first step in selling out the republic. Even if this were the case, surely

Kazakhastan wasn't *less* exploited in the past seventy years? All our raw materials were exported to other republics, but the people, the workers who extracted these resources received nothing in exchange. I have already explained the problems of the miners who were simply forced into their desperate actions. Of course, you have to keep your wits about you when you deal with western businessmen. None of them is going to give us something for nothing. We have to find mutually beneficial options. But we can't get anywhere with a closed economy. Our experience has already shown that no matter how many walls you put up around your household, if you don't run your little farm well, you'll end up losing your shirt no matter what.

We make no secret of our strategy in working with foreign businesses. Our final goal is to enter the world market with finished products, not raw materials. But today we need some part of the money we can get from selling raw materials in order to buy consumer goods. But we don't intend to spend all the money. That would be foolish. The rest of it should be used to invest primarily in processing industries.

We can learn a lot from South Korea, which began introducing a market economy without having any natural resources. But first it allowed foreign businesses into its markets while training its own workers and engineers. At first many enterprises belonged to foreign companies and corporations. But the state used all the money earned to produce export goods. In a relatively short time it began exporting about sixty percent of its products. Gradually the country regained its enterprises. For instance, in 1989 South Korea had 15 billion dollars in hard currency, and spent 10 billion of it to increase wages (by 26 per cent) while promoting democratic reforms.

Of course any experience, even the best, cannot be copied mechanically. Life always has a way of presenting new problems that require serious adjustments. Much depends on the traditions of political and public affairs, and the mentality of the people. I would like to point out once again that Korea started its transition to a market economy without any resources, whereas Kazakhstan has enormous potential in this area. If this potential is not properly utilized, we won't have any alternative but to feed people again with promises of a better life in a "bright future."

CHAPTER SIX

Sons of the Times

I realize full well the pitfalls in trying to understand a past or present phenomenon, to remember one's own life, and analyze the experience gained over a lifetime. It's necessary to go into details about one's life, but it's possible to drown in those details, to mistakenly think something's important when really it's secondary, to be subjective and allow emotions and passions to get the upper hand. It is especially hard to talk about people you knew personally. It's one thing when the memories are only good. But all of us understand that life is complicated and sometimes it's necessary to stand up not only against something, but against someone, that is, a specific person. Even if we are convinced that someone deserves serious criticism, do we always have the right to do that publicly, to ask the people to be the final judge?

There's no simple answer to that question. That is why I don't particularly want to go into much detail about the complicated relations I have had with many well-known people. If I do take the responsibility of characterizing someone it is because otherwise it is impossible to understand what I consider the most important events, and the causes of many complex phenomena in recent years. I am honestly wary that I might be mistaken for those who are so eager to expose and accuse others, and who despise any page of our past history.

Today it is common to refer to the experience and tradition of civilized states. Since in these cases what is meant by "civilized" is the capitalist countries exclusively, I would like to talk about my impressions from travelling on business in the western world. For instance, in the United States when I met various ranking leaders, I noted that in the offices of mayors I would see the portraits of all their predecessors. It makes no difference whether the current mayor agrees with the political views of these predecessors. A mayor might even think one of them should have been electrocuted!

The United States has another tradition as well. Every president, after leaving his post, begins creating a library of sorts. Both personal and public funds are used for this purpose. Such libraries are not only collections of books, but rich and interesting museums, cultural centres that are visited by numerous people. When I went to the Truman Library in Kansas City I couldn't help but ask this question: "Here you are paying honor to this president when he was the one at the end of World War II who dropped an atomic bomb on civilians?" The reply was that dropping the atomic bomb was, of course, a terrible act, but it was part of history; also, it shouldn't be forgotten what Truman did for the American nation and state.

This was their calm and considered approach. Respect for history, no matter how bitter it is, in my opinion, is characteristic of any modern civilized society. In Italy, for instance, there aren't many people who sympathize with the former fascist dictator. However, to this day monuments to Mussolini still stand, and nobody thinks anything of it. Recently I went to Madrid in the delegation that travelled with Mikhail Gorbachev. And I saw there that no one was desecrating the monument to the dictator Franco.

Somewhere I read that people who don't respect their history don't respect themselves. Unfortunately, our own conduct convincingly bears out and illustrates this truth. As we slander our entire past we sprinkle ashes over our head and repent about everything possible. We scream to the whole world that we can't do anything, that we're ready to bow to anything foreign.

History doesn't need procurators or lawyers; it needs researchers. A concern for history is the best guarantee that today and tomorrow we won't repeat any new tragic mistakes. I think it's time now to break this permanent chain of criticizing everything and everyone. Those who are particularly vociferous forget that, based on one of our worst traditions, tomorrow *they* may be the object of condemnation.

The year before last Kunayev suffered a great loss—his wife died. He had no children so he lost an important source of support. I knew his deceased wife quite well. She always helped her husband as a traditional housewife, and protected him from unpleasant difficulties. To lose such a person is a heavy blow to anyone. An hour after I heard the sad news I went to his home.

I remember how he got up out of his chair with such difficulty, like an old man. According to our tradition we embraced each other and I expressed my sympathies. When we sat down (we weren't alone in the house) he began to talk about the past. It was clear that he was talking about things he had been thinking about a lot, because in such times it's impossible to be insincere. He said that when you're in such a high post it's inevitable to make serious mistakes. He said he thought we should forgive each other and not harbour bad feelings. When he talked about the new leadership, he looked me in the eyes, and said he supported everything we were doing. "The people understand and support you," he commented. "I bear no hard feelings against anyone." Kunayev reconfirmed this in a recent interview in the republic's youth newspaper.

I also thought about the mistakes that I had made in those difficult times. After all, in times of harsh confrontation we sometimes lose sight of what we all have in common as human beings even if we are big political opponents. Is deep sorrow the only thing that can reconcile us? Too often, in political fighting, in the heat of our ambitions, we lose this natural sense of human unity, and thereby create divisions throughout society, and generate confrontation. What kind of consolidation can we hope for if even in our daily affairs we allow politics to divide us into democrats, party bosses, liberals, and conservatives?

Kunayev was far from the simple figure he's made out to be by many. He was extremely erudite, and most importantly, he understood Kazakhstan very well, its traditions, and the mentality of the people. It is absolutely wrong to explain his prestige merely by pointing to Brezhnev's support. The main reason for Kunayev's tragedy was, in my opinion, the belief that developed over the decades that the party leadership was incapable of wrong-doing and was almighty. Authoritarianism sooner or later seeps into anyone who climbs to the top of the pyramid of power. Someone with authoritarian power feels best when subordinates are fearful of him. Kunayev's favourite credo was, "To be obedient your employees should be afraid of you."

Everything that went on in the upper echelons in Moscow was copied to the minutest detail in Alma-Ata, all the way down to the local regions. The same traditions, ethics, habits, whether it was a passion for hunting, for wearing lots of medals, or for pompous anniversary celebrations that wasted an enormous amount of energy and money. There's a saying in Russia that a fish rots from the head; it applies to this situation exactly. The degeneration in the party was from the top on down, and this was what brought about the stagnation in society.

I can't remember one year in which I was able to deal only with serious matters, with actual work. I was spending a significant amount of time arranging for celebrations, one after another. In 1980, it was the 60th anniversary of Kazakhstan and Brezhnev's visit; in 1981 it was the 250th anniversary of Kazakhstan's voluntary entry into Russia, then the anniversary of the virgin lands. All this was done with great extravagance.

January 12, 1982, was Kunayev's seventieth anniversary. We found out in the morning from a telegram signed by Chernenko that on his birthday Kunayev was awarded the Order of the October Revolution. We had just gathered to go and wish our chief a happy birthday when we were told to stay where we were and wait for further instructions. At the end of the day the news came that Kunayev was given his third Hero of Socialist Labor award and the Order of Lenin. Apparently Kunayev's people in the apparatus had managed in a few hours to get Brezhnev to add a resolution to the draft document that Chernenko had drawn up. It was just a formality to get another Directive of the Presidium of the USSR Supreme Soviet. Shcherbitsky, Aliev, and Rashidov already had two Hero of Socialist Labor awards. When Kunayev received a third medal it boosted his importance significantly.

Incidentally, it was quite common in those days to hint about getting a medal. During an anniversary or a successful harvest all sorts of people received awards in the Central Committee and other leadership bodies, everyone including clerks, cleaning people, and chauffeurs. The problem was not that their work didn't deserve recognition, but that this practice was not an objective way to evaluate the results of work. Ultimately no attention was paid to promoting reasonable motivation for conscientious work.

There was a period when many thought that the administrative-command system would crack any minute. The first alarm went off when Yuri Andropov became general secretary of the party. People in the party began talking about stagnation in the economy, about the decline in development, about the need for greater discipline, an end to abuses, and making everything subject to criticism.

By this time the bureaucratic system in the apparatus at all levels, including the CPSU Central Committee, had organized a powerful defense mechanism against the numerous complaints and requests of the people. One resolution after another was passed to deal with this problem, and some, as we well remember, were very strong sounding, yet they were nothing more than camouflage. Contacts were so tight that the only information that reached Moscow about our republic was what our leadership thought necessary.

Under Andropov all written appeals were strictly investigated. When serious problems and illegal activities were uncovered in Uzbekistan it became clear that our own leaders in Alma-Ata and many other regions were getting very worried. However after the first "shakeup" the local leadership found a way to adapt to this unpleasant turn of events. They decided to let out the steam that had collected among the people by focusing all their efforts on finding individuals in movie theatres, stores, hairdressers, and even bathhouses when they were supposed to be at work.

I don't agree with those who claim that Andropov's early death, and the subsequent interruption in planned political reforms, made a difference in the path this country has taken. Clearly, if we had continued the reform process with that authoritarian approach we would have inevitably reached a dead end.

It's true that when Andropov died life returned to the way it had always been. I was at the full-scale meeting of the CPSU Central Committee when Konstantin Chernenko was elected General Secretary. Everyone saw his condition and were indignant that at the 26th Party Congress he couldn't even pronounce the names of the people he was nominating to the Central Committee. Everyone knew him as a bureaucrat who had spent his entire career in the apparatus, mainly doing paperwork. The old forces were able to keep things as they were, but it was evident that their hold on power couldn't last forever.

I recall very well my conversation with Gorbachev when I was recommended to become the Chair of the Kazakhstan Council of Ministers. We had a long and serious conversation. Gorbachev said he appreciated how my career had developed and my position on many issues. Afterwards he asked:

"What do you think, do you have a backbone?"

I didn't understand at first what he meant.

"Difficult times lie ahead," he explained. "There will be an assault, a fight. It won't be easy."

According to protocol I had to meet with Chernenko after that conversation. I had to wait in my hotel room indefinitely for the call about my appointment with the General Secretary. I waited three days. Finally the call came: "The General Secretary cannot see you now, he's ill. Go back home."

A week later I was called to Moscow again. Again I waited in my hotel room. On the third day I received the call: "Keep waiting, the General Secretary is not in Moscow; he's probably resting in his country residence." A day later I was told the General Secretary could not see me, and to go back to Alma-Ata.

The third time I went to Moscow I had the meeting. Yegor Ligachev took me to Chernenko. Naturally I had prepared myself thoroughly for the meeting. I wanted to look good, to I tried to foresee every question I might be asked about the republic. When we entered the office Chernenko was sitting in a chair looking tired and expressionless. He seemed quite ill. He was all grey, there was no colour in his face, and he stretched out a limp hand.

Ligachev began telling him about me, reminding him that I would be the youngest prime minister in any of the republics. Chernenko sat quietly, breathing hard. When Ligachev finished his monologue he finally asked the first and only question:

"How old is he?"

He's going on forty-four. He'll be the youngest prime minister," Ligachev repeated.

Suddenly Chernenko rose and walked toward me, but collapsed and a young sturdy fellow nearby barely caught him.

"When you return give my regards to our comrades."

The meeting, which left a terrible impression, was over.

After such meetings, you can't help but thinking about the consequences of such a person being at the helm of a major country. It was clear that a man in such shape was incapable of having any serious influence on developments. It meant someone had something to gain from a General Secretary who was merely a symbol of power, who would just allow others to do what they wanted. For instance, we knew from Kunayev that there was a special secret resolution of the Politburo that enabled the elderly members to work less hours every day, and gave them long weekends, starting Friday. That is why they weren't particularly overworked and, as a rule, on Thursdays everyone left for their country houses to breathe the fresh air, and hunt in special areas. On Monday they would return to Moscow. That was how local leaders also conducted their lives. Their only duties were to be present from time to time at meetings, sometimes visit a local area, and turn up once in a while in the mass media to show they weren't asleep, that they *were* our leaders. There were similar ceremonial positions locally. For instance, being the chair of the presidium of a republic's Supreme Soviet was not a bad way to spend one's old age. In 1984, when S. N. Imashev died, the elderly B. A. Ashimov, who was the chair of the Council of Ministers, replaced Imashev as the chair of the Supreme Soviet's Presidium. As a result of this simple rotation, I became the head of the republic's government.

My predecessor, as many other leaders, followed one principle, and that was to keep everything quiet and peaceful. The less you troubled others, the more peaceful your own life was. The trick was to look up often to make sure you were pleasing the highest leadership. This was a sure way to stay in power. Incidentally, the former chair of the Council of Ministers was also decorated with the golden star of Hero of Socialist Labour.

Our own 'expanse'.

In the industrial town of TAMIRTAU appeared a new 'NURSULTAN'.

Yesterday's worker – today's President.

In the White House – Washington – 1992.

Meeting in the ancient country of Turkistan.

The family of the President.

An improvement in Soviet-Austrian relations.

cosmic crews in Bikonur.

Meeting with
countrymen.

Russia-Kazakhstan
together forever.

Golden Kazakhstan.

/hite House – 1992.

Meeting with
Helmut Kohl.

Meeting with Mitterand.

Nursultan Nazarbaev

I already mentioned the situation I inherited in agriculture. I knew all about the traditional ways in which industrial problems were settled since the time I became Secretary of the Central Committee in charge of industry. These intricate methods for getting around the plans had worn me out completely. I had to go through the same agony when we undertook the development of the oil fields on the peninsula of Buzachi and Tenghiz, the Karachaganak gas deposits, the construction of the Ekibastuz cascade of electric power stations and the tire plant in Chimkent, the expansion of the Novodzhambul phosphorous plant, improvements in the Alga chemical plant, and various light industry plants.

However, any serious attempt I made to reveal one or another cause of the negative phenomena that had accumulated over the years only alienated Kunayev from me. Any step, even if it couldn't be interpreted in any way as criticism of Kunayev's personal qualities, was still seen as an attack on his authority.

Only later I realized why such fierce resistance was put up against anyone who tried to make a difference and in 1985 I wholeheartedly welcomed the announcement of reforms at the April Plenary Session of the CPSU Central Committee. Although the top leadership of the administrative-command system proclaimed for decades that they did everything in the interests of society and the people, what they really cared about most was to strengthen their own positions. Therefore anything that could make even the slightest crack in the system that they controlled was a threat to the personal welfare of specific people.

Much has been written and said about the role the April Plenary Session played in our country. Unfortunately it's necessary to take the time to remind people of what should be obvious. I am amazed at how much our evaluations have changed of what were unquestionably historic developments. I am absolutely convinced that there was no other force in our society capable of making such a decisive turn in a new direction but the party and its healthy core in the leadership that had its support from the rank and file. I think it's too simplistic to regard that healthy process as a "revolution from above". Any attempts by the top leadership to engineer a "coup d'etat" was doomed to fail, or, at best, would have left the system intact. However it was clear from the outset that the undertaking charted in April of 1985 would have strong and broad support at the lower levels. That did occur. No one doubted the role of the party that had decisively broken with the flawed traditions of stagnation.

At first, even the advocates of more radical, and even extremist measures did not question the role of the CPSU. I remember how the public welcomed the book "No Other Alternative", which contained the most daring ideas of the first years of perestroika. In the foreword, the editor and one of the authors, Yuri Afanasiev, noted that the book was about the future of the new policies of the CPSU, about what and who were blocking their implementation. But the ink hadn't even dried on the book when most of the authors began attacking those same "new policies" in an attempt to remove the party from the political scene and criticize indiscriminately all members of the party. According to the strange logic of these people, the party, that had started perestroika, was also in the way of it working. In my opinion the healthy forces in the party were primarily in the way of those authoritarian leaders who wanted to look like democrats. It is no accident that at a critical turning point the struggle of ideas was replaced by a struggle of ambitions among a small group of people who also claim to have a monopoly on the truth.

Some people have a simplistic view of how the resolutions of the April Plenary Session affected the party. Many think that after the plenary session all that was required was just a wave of the wand to improve the situation in local areas. I remember how it took a whole year just for the healthy forces in the Kazakh Communist Party to speak openly against the old leadership's efforts to keep things the way they were. This first took place in February 1986 at the republic's 16th Party Congress. After discussing the Central Committee report that was presented in the traditional spirit by Kunayev, I was supposed to give my report on economic and social development between 1986 and 1990, and until 2000. To give a complete picture of the situation in agriculture and industry in the republic, I'll quote from the actual report and what I said about the negative problems:

"In a number of industries the targets of the last five-year plan have not been met. Growth in output and productivity in general were lower by 3.6 and 4.6 points, respectively. One out of four enterprises has not filled all the orders that it contracted, and the yield per unit of assets has fallen by 15 percent. Out of 334 facilities built in the past 9 years, nearly half are still not producing at capacity. Agriculture has also not kept to its commitments. It has not provided the state with 18.5 million tons of grain that it promised, and has not reached targets for any of the livestock. In construction 2.7 billion rubles of capital investments have not been used.

"These problems are largely because certain ministers, chairs of committees and local governments were not able to change their methods in accordance with the approaches charted at the April Plenary Session of the CPSU Central Committee. They often spent their efforts not on strengthening discipline, but on finding all sorts of reasons for adjusting planned targets. Instead of actively working to make fundamental changes they were satisfied with average statistical indicators and accomplishments by some subordinates.

"The old style of boasting about individual successes and the local leaders has not been overcome and has negative consequences. All this was possible also because the republic's leadership has not discouraged these unacceptable methods.

"The leadership of the Academy of Sciences, headed by its president, Askar Kunayev, is beset by inertia. It has not been able to mobilize the republic's academic forces to resolve fundamental problems within the sciences and in the economy. That is why none of the academy's institutes was included in the nation's industrial scientific and technological complexes, and in the whole last five-year-plan period not one license for an invention was signed. It is also troubling that last year the economic efficiency of one technology that was developed and introduced in the republic declined by half since 1980, and out of 76 proposals made by the academy of sciences, only 5 were accepted in the state plan, and only 9 in the plans of ministries and agencies.

"Today at this congress it is necessary to say frankly that the republic's Academy of Sciences is an organization not subject to criticism. Apparently that is why the Academy's president attends neither meetings of the Council of Ministers, nor various important commissions. He is essentially not doing his job. I think that it is time to compel him to do his duty.

". . . As before, farming is done unsystematically on one-fifth of the cultivated land. Irrigated farming is still not organized well enough. Every year 40,000 to 80,000 hectares of land are not watered . . . The increase in livestock is not in keeping with the fodder available. And productivity of the livestock, which is most important, is not taken into account.

"In 1985 the situation with milk improved somewhat. Each cow gave 1,993 kilograms of milk. But this was the level in 1970! The average weight of meat from each head of cattle was 344 kilograms, or 60 kilograms less than in 1980, and in the Kustanai, Taldy-Kurgan and Semipalatinsk regions the decrease was from 70 to 109 kilograms. The average weight of the meat from sheep was 3 kilograms less, and the amount of wool was 400 grams less . . . We can't speak of any successes in livestock breeding. On the contrary, we have slipped back. We have fallen short of planned targets by 385,000 tons of meat in live weight, 152,000 tons of milk, and nearly 6,000 tons of wool.

"In the past ten years capital investments in rural areas amounted to over 32 billion rubles, production funds rose 1.8 times, and supplies of fertilizers 2.4 times, but the gross output of agriculture increased only by 23 percent. And productivity has not risen.

"Between 1981 and 1984, the cost of producing a centner of milk increased by 7 rubles, a centner of beef increased by 71, a centner of pork by 31, and a centner of lamb by 32 rubles. How could the cost *not* rise considering that last year an investigation by the Council of Ministers discovered that on one-third of the farms in the Kzyl-Orda, Turgai, and Aktyubinsk regions less livestock was sold to the government than planned and some livestock was not even reported? In these regions alone the privately-owned livestock maintained illegally in the publicly-owned herds amounted to 23,000 heads of cattle, 130,000 sheep, and nearly 10,000 horses. Around 400 sheep owned by local officials and specialists were kept in the herds of the Zhenishkekum State Farm in the Kzyl-Orda Region.

"Due to waste and theft, in the past five years the republic's state farms had a deficit of nearly 120,000 heads of cattle over 1.7 million sheep, and 42,000 horses and 42,000 pigs.

"It is especially alarming that these outrageous facts were not evaluated as such in local party and government bodies, nor in the former Ministry of Agriculture. This is apparently because no reaction to the report made by the Committee of People's Control was forthcoming from the bureau or the Secretariat of the Central Committee, even though over 26 million rubles were lost in these regions due to waste and theft over a 14 month period.

"We still have the problem in our republic of unplanned construction . . . Often the reason for these building projects is that local officials, with no regard for regulations, insist on erecting "prestigious" facilities. This practice, condemned by the CPSU Central Committee, has been common in the Chimkent, Karaganda, and East Kazakhstan regions. In Alma-Ata the former leadership of the regional and city party committees forced the rapid construction of the Central State Museum that cost 9.3 million rubles at a time when materials and labor were in short supply for the construction of housing and other necessary municipal buildings. There were periods when the number of workers on this "vitally" necessary project was as much as 1,000. Although the museum was finished in June of last year, it was opened to the public just recently.

"Similar methods were used to build other "prestigious" facilities in the capital. Undoubtedly, Alma-Ata needs these buildings. But first we should have built the housing that was planned for this five-year period; instead, we fell short of the plan by 115,000 square meters.

"As you know from the daily Pravda, in Saryagach of the Chimkent Region, a luxury hotel with imported furniture, carpets, fixtures, and equipment was built illegally. It was built hastily by the Chimkentselstroy-25 Trust that put the paperwork through as though the structure was an ordinary twelve-unit apartment house. When the time came to take responsibility for the deception, Dzhandosov, the chair of the Chimkent regional executive committee, said that he didn't know anything about the project. Perhaps he's right, many such facilities were built under the nose of the regional leadership. It's no surprise that one of these facilities that cost over half a million rubles could simply vanish. One of the first vacationers in this hotel was the chair of the State Construction Committee, Bektemisov, whose duty was to prevent such building projects.

"Some comrades think it's disgraceful for them to live in ordinary homes. They want something special—higher ceilings and more floor space. This was the approach of the Dzhambul regional executive committee that built a six-unit house for the local leadership. Isn't this the kind of arrogance the party is decisively fighting today? Unfortunately many local officials and managers were infected by these same ambitions to underscore their superiority. They developed traits that were totally incompatible with the image of a communist, and so they lost the respect of the workers, and ultimately their jobs. It is also relevant to mention the country residences and luxurious estates that were built ostensibly for special guests, although they would stay empty for months in expectation of their rare occupants. The working class from which many of these officials came has the right to be indignant about this kind of aristocratic behaviour.

". . . It is also necessary to raise the issue of social justice in allotting apartments. This is the sacred duty of primarily local government bodies. The first secretaries of city party committees and chairs of city executive committees in Kokchetav, Kzyl-Orda, the chair of the Dzhambul city executive committee and a number of others were dismissed for having flagrantly violated housing legislation.

"Major violations were also committed in Alma-Ata. An investigation showed that in the past two and a half years the city's regional executive committees provided only one percent of the capital's housing to people on legitimate waiting lists. It wasn't hard at all for the chair of the Alma-Ata regional executive committee, Belyakov, to give his three-room apartment to his children while moving into a new four-room apartment with his wife. Abenov, who was chair of the East Kazakhstan regional executive committee since 1982, never gave up his residence permit in Alma-Ata, yet was assigned an apartment in Ust-Kamenogorsk. It would take a lot of time for me to enumerate all these examples. I wouldn't even mention these cases if they weren't so widespread.

"All this is going on at a time when the capital has nearly 3,000 families with disabled members, war veterans, and families of killed servicemen who live in substandard housing. Many of these people have been on the waiting lists for more than twenty years. Typically these officials try to get apartments for their relatives in the centre of town and in new buildings with the best floor plans and interior decorating. They make these arrangements in all sorts of illegal ways. All this demands a special investigation.

". . . The situation was especially intolerable in the consumer cooperatives where it became common practice to embezzle cooperative money during the leadership of Tanekeev, head of the board of Kazpotrebsoyuz. The total amount of money embezzled in the four and a half years of the previous five-year period was over 20 million rubles and over 46 million in unproductive spending and losses.

"In the Dzhezkazgan city cooperative system the embezzlement amounted to 768,000 rubles. Last year alone in the Chimkent regional cooperative union the embezzlement amounted to 1,400,000 rubles. The chair of the Alma-Ata cooperative union, Gorgopko, was dismissed for flagrant violations. Similar outrages were committed in other regions as well. It is necessary to combat these practices decisively. These problems were reported to law enforcement agencies long ago, but unfortunately they did not stop the violations at the outset. In some cases law enforcement officials were involved themselves in these illegal activities."

I did not mention in my report anything about Kunayev. Furthermore, I hoped that by raising these issues so forthrightly I would shake up the inert leaders and stop their activities that would sooner or later defeat the first secretary. After all, despite the serious differences we had, I never lost my basic human respect for him. We were conditioned from an early age throughout the republic to honor our leader. Kunayev's portraits were in every office, and even in bomb shelters. Besides, I was often reminded that were it not for him I would not have become a Central Committee secretary or chair of the Council of Ministers.

My report managed to reach the delegates. I was interrupted on several occasions with applause, and when I finished I got a standing ovation. I say this without false modesty because just a few months before, as I already mentioned, my attempt to raise these issues frankly was stonewalled. Now the situation had changed radically; people believed that the reforms were irreversible. However, when I left the podium to go back to the presidium I was struck by Kunayev's hard, expressionless face.

A harassment campaign against me began that very day. I don't want to go into the details about the unethical methods used in that massive assault, especially since all that is in the distant past, and I know that many of the participants sincerely regretted their actions. In the three weeks between the 16th Kazakh Communist Party Congress and the 27th CPSU Congress, 53 complaints were filed against me and every possible commission thoroughly investigated the charges.

Hard times began for me. How did I survive the experience? First of all because of the principled support I had from my comrades who believed in and were behind the reforms. At the same 16th Party Congress similar critical presentations were made following mine by a secretary of the Kazakh Central Committee, Z. Kamalidenov, secretaries of regional party committees, E. N. Auelbekov and the late Yu. N. Trofimov. However there were those who accused us of slandering the great son of the Kazakh people. It seemed sometimes that everything could go back to how it was, because Kunayev was re-elected First Secretary of the republic's Party Central Committee, and subsequently made a member of the Politburo at the 27th CPSU Congress.

Despite all this, the ice had been broken. My position also had support among Politburo members, and particularly Mikhail Gorbachev. After Kunayev raised the issue of dismissing me from my post as chair of the Council of Ministers and several statements by him that I was trying to get him out of the way to take over myself, Gorbachev suggested that the whole situation be discussed at a meeting of the Politburo in my presence. Kunayev declined the offer.

It would be wrong of me not to mention the firm and consistent position taken on this matter by Yegor Ligachev. In our wholesale criticism of the period of stagnation we have managed to hang labels on all the leaders, calling some of them democrats and others conservatives. But since we have begun building a democratic law-governed society, we must show respect for people who stand up for what they believe. It's another matter whether society shares the same beliefs. But one thing is certain: Ligachev did not go from one extreme to another. He spoke openly about how he understood the social and political processes, and defended his convictions. I think he deserves credit for this. Besides, we are often witnesses to unusual developments today. For instance, after organizing a real smear campaign against Ligachev, the democratic press is now happily publishing his memoirs.

Having made this small detour off the subject, I would like to stress again how important it was for me to have Ligachev's support in this difficult and uncompromising struggle to improve the situation in Kazakhstan. Ligachev shared my position completely when I appealed to the CPSU Central Committee and personally to Gorbachev with my view of the situation and a request to send a commission to the republic to investigate the problems. I had no other alternative in that situation which I remember today like a nightmare. In that same appeal I also asked to be relieved of my duties as chair of the Council of Ministers, since it was impossible in that atmosphere for me to continue my job.

When you talk about the well-known leaders of the recent period you probably realize that many of the party officials who worked in the past with them are now some of the party's most militant critics, exposing all the ills, both genuine and imaginary. What's your opinion of this phenomenon?

I don't think that any change of convictions should be regarded as treachery. After all, many of us were captives of dogmatic interpretations of Marxism-Leninism, and believed blindly in some "pure" idea. If the misconceptions were sincere then why can't the enlightenment be sincere as well? I believe that a new and creative analysis of the theoretical works of Marx and Lenin, a rejection of the dogmatism of Stalinism, can help us understand much about the real essence of socialism. We have already talked about whether what we had in this country was socialism. I agree with the economists and social scientists who believe, for instance, that for the past seven decades we had what is referred to as a mobilized economy. Let's look back again at our past—one mobilization after another. People were mobilized to fight in the civil war, to rebuild from the ruins of war, and to push forward industrialization. After World War II the people were mobilized to rebuild the economy, develop the virgin lands, and to work on the major Young Communist League construction projects. This is without even mentioning the continual mobilizations to reach planned targets. Essentially we were always telling the individual what to do. All the dictators became so used to this power they had over the people that they didn't want to give it up.

While we were mobilizing people by using high-sounding dogmas and not facing economic problems head on, the whole world advanced toward higher living standards. Was there any socialism in our economic relations? The social scientists can debate that. I believe that we can answer this question only by creating a pluralist economy, and a truly democratic and free society. That's why I don't think we should evaluate people based on their adherence to one or another idea. We have many leaders who are used to changing their opinions according to which way the wind is blowing. But we shouldn't pin labels on them either. Let it be on their conscience.

Market relations are founded on entrepreneurship. Money is a pivotal matter in the process of building these relations. Many think that pragmatism will make people more materialistic and will erode their spiritual qualities.

The paradox is that we have always considered ourselves materialists. After all, hasn't our philosophy always been that the material world shapes our consciousness, our thinking? We have criticized all possible idealistic conceptions in the bourgeois world. In practice the "idealists" have been dealing with problems of the real world, and our "materialists" have been building one utopian idea after another. Our idealism, separated from life, has penetrated all aspects of social relations, and has disrupted the economy. Instead of paying people according to their work, we had a system of levelling. We kept people from feeling they were masters of their lives and therefore inculcated parasitism among the millions. As for the cultural values that critics of the market economy seem so worried about, they were torn out by the roots, and trampled on the ground. Whatever we did have, we sent abroad because we couldn't afford to nurture it here.

It is time for us to look squarely at what we have in reality. We either persecuted entrepreneurial people or waved them away like irritating flies. As a result we lost millions of innovations and inventions that sometimes had no equal in the world. Most importantly we ruined people's lives. For instance, the whole country has learned about the tragic fate of I. N. Khudenko, an agricultural innovator. A. A. Knyaginin, a man from Semipalatinsk, endured terrible suffering, including imprisonment, for creating a whole complex of fodder production enabling the industrialization of sheep breeding. Incidentally, he is now a representative in the Kazakh parliament. As chair of the Council of Ministers I was involved in the case of N. F. Zhalybin and his two sons, Nikolai and Oleg, who developed light weight structures for sheep-folds, hothouses, storage for farm products, and repair shops. Ordinary sheep-folds were priced at 300,000 rubles, but the Zhalybins could make them for 40,000. Nevertheless the brothers could not fight the bureaucratic redtape and the wasteful economic system that preferred higher prices over quality. Now the Zhalybin structures are used throughout the republic. But it took tremendous efforts. A common feeling is that the people will not accept a division between rich and poor. But what alternative do we offer — equality in poverty? After all, 60 million people are living below the poverty line.

As for the cultural life of our people, for the first time in seven decades it has been liberated from the dictates of ideology and the tyranny of a totalitarian regime. It's only in recent years that the Kazakhs, like most other peoples in this country, have been able to discover their multi-faceted heritage that was created by the best of our people and mercilessly murdered in the thirties. Since then the great works of talented Kazakh writers were banned because they didn't follow the principles of socialist realism, because they were religious and nationalistic. These criticisms are familiar ideological labels.

Perestroika has significantly restored our cultural heritage. In the future we will not overlook the renewal of our culture and that of all peoples. Now, for instance, we are actively supporting the various new cultural centres in the republic for the Russian, German, Korean, and a number of other peoples. The government of the republic has allocated an enormous new building to house a united multi-ethnic cultural center. Unfortunately, many important undertakings in this area lack government financial support and can be accomplished only with voluntary help. To some degree we can rely on the republic's cultural foundation that is now being organized. But this will not settle the problem. After all, we have to build a qualitatively new material base, finance the construction of theaters, music schools, dance studios, art schools, libraries, and other facilities that we sorely lack. Our old economy was a failure in this respect as well. And so you see that again we get back to economic problems, and see that the old economic system will not preserve our cultural values.

CHAPTER SEVEN

The Force of Inertia

Our contradictory times have prompted an amazing paradoxical phenomenon. On the one hand, it is unquestionable that perestroika has had a positive impact on all aspects of our society. It is no exaggeration that the people share a common understanding of the need and inevitability of radical changes. On the other hand, attempts are made to blame perestroika for the country's profound political and economic crisis. The memory is still clear of those times when we praised to the skies the "architects of perestroika." Today we are already beginning to call these people to account, accusing them of all sorts of mistakes and failures.

So it seems that the fresh April wind not only improved the air in our common home, but also gave its vulnerable inhabitants new ailments. I don't want to raise again the issue of our tendency as a society to swing from one extreme to another and condemn yesterday's idols while raising new ones on pedestals only to go the way of their predecessors. At the same time we should understand the reasons why this illness has recurred of late. The reasons can be divided into objective and subjective.

The objective reasons were related to the very nature of our political and socio-economic development until 1985. I think anyone would have to agree that most of our troubles were already inevitable by that time. It is absurd to maintain that we had everything we needed before. Throughout 1985 and 1986 warnings were made that the country was on the verge of a crisis. Everyone agreed with that. But we weren't able to prevent the crisis. Not only did the situation worsen catastrophically in the economy, but totally unexpected phenomena developed in other spheres. Five or six years ago none of us could have predicted such profound inter-ethnic conflicts that would make dubious the future of the Union. I do not intend to take on the major responsibility of analyzing all the reasons for our problems. I think it's possible in these stormy times while history is in the making only to record the facts accurately. A quest for cause and effect relationships between events and phenomena when political passions are at the boiling point can only lead to serious new misconceptions that the most objective observer cannot avoid. At the same time we can't afford to ignore the fact that the nature of many trends is already obvious.

One of the serious contradictions in the process of perestroika is the deep conflict between the Union republics and the central government, which is reflected in the "parade of declarations of independence" and the "war of laws." Of course this is happening because the central government underestimated the growing sense of ethnic identity among the peoples that was exploited by different political trends and organizations. Incidentally this is another serious historical lesson that should steer us away from narrow pragmatic thinking and press us to achieve a qualitatively higher level of thinking about historical processes and the prospects for development. The trend in today's world toward economic integration and the weakening of barriers between states. This is accompanied by an increasing concern among peoples for their ethnic and national identity, for a resurrection of their cultural and historical traditions, which is often attended by excessive nationalism and negative consequences.

Getting back to our domestic problems, I think that the reasons for our inter-ethnic crisis are more prosaic, but just as important. One of the causes is the great inertia of the administrative-command methods used by the leadership. This was especially true in the early stage of political reforms in Kazakhstan and set the republic on a critical course with dire consequences. Ultimately the very logic of the developments rejected this inertia. Today when conflicts and violence are sparked by ethnic minorities, many have begun to see the 1986 riots in Alma-Ata as an ordinary episode in the kaleidoscope of recent events. At that time, however, those events promoted many articles and comments. But probably not everyone remembers that a special resolution of the ORSU Central Committee condemned what was referred to as Kazakh nationalism. Even fewer people know that somewhat later, following our insistent demands, the resolution was declared a mistake. (Unfortunately that mistake did not prevent the leadership of the party and government from making more mistakes of the same kind.) In early December 1986, I returned to Alma-Ata after visiting the oil and gas fields of Kazakhstan together with Nikolai Ryzhkov, Chair of the USSR Council of Ministers. We were met by Kunayev who had just returned from Moscow and said that he was officially retiring. It wasn't clear why he seemed so cheerful about that. However I understood right away when I found out that Moscow had already chosen his replacement, which meant that essentially nothing had changed. Apparently the central government still considered the republic its domain and saw no need to consult with anyone, so it just went ahead and made its own choice. Not even the Central Committee of the Communist Party of Kazakhstan was informed about who its first secretary would be.

On December 15, one day before the full-scale meeting of the Kazakhstan Central Committee was to discuss organizational matters, we learned that Gennadi Kolbin had just arrived from Moscow to replace Kunayev. Kolbin, who was then the first secretary of the Ulyanovsk regional party committee, was accompanied by G. P. Razumovsky, secretary of the CPSU Central Committee in charge of personnel.

Such an approach to this crucial issue, essentially the future of Kazakhstan, shocked the members of the republic's party bureau. Everyone was in a trance over the fact that no one had even thought of at least discussing the candidate at a meeting of the bureau, even just as a formality. Actually it would've been hard for us even to discuss the matter because none of us knew Kolbin. That was the background of our full-scale Central Committee meeting which lasted exactly eighteen minutes. Everyone raised their hands in agreement, and Kolbin became first secretary. Once again we saw the triumph of mindless obedience to Moscow and barracks mentality: "We're just soldiers in the party." No one even contemplated the consequences, which were just around the corner.

The very next day a group of young people began gathering on the square in front of the Central Committee building. At first two hundred people arrived with posters, but the crowd continued to grow. Kolbin called us to his office to discuss the situation. He asked two members of the bureau, including myself and S. Mukashev, chair of the Presidium of the republic's Supreme Soviet, to go out and talk to the people. No one regretted that Kunayev had retired. Some of the posters said: "Each [group of] people needs its own leader," "We need a Kazakh leader," "Down with dictates," "We have perestroka, but where's democracy?" "We're for a Leninist nationalitles policy." No reasonable person could disagree with these slogans. The people were in a peaceful mood. We had only one question to answer: "Why wasn't someone local chosen?" But we couldn't give a satisfactory explanation. Then the demonstrators started walking down the streets of Alma-Ata carrying their signs.

In everyone's life there are moments when suddenly a crucial choice has to be made, a choice between what is familiar, comfortable, and what is unpredictably complex or painful. A person faced with such a dilemma who does not conform to the circumstances, who remains true to himself, ultimately gains. When the people began their march into town I realized that I faced such a dilemma—either take a stand or return to the Central Committee offices. The latter seemed an inexcusable betrayal of the people who were right. I went with them, at the head of the crowd.

The march through the town lasted three hours. After making a big circle the people returned to the square. After lunch the numbers increased. We were joined by students, workers, the intelligentsia. The next day the demonstration was resumed. Everyone knows how it ended. On December 18, the crowd was dispersed by force. I don't want to discuss whether this measure was necessary or justified. Something had to be done because tensions were rising; hooligans and extremists joined the crowd. The main issue is that the whole incident could have been prevented. Unfortunately it wasn't. Everyone was powerless to resolve the conflict that erupted between the government and the people. It didn't help matters that Moscow sent to the new first secretary's "aid" a whole group of prominent representatives of the central government, including the deputy chair of the KGB, and the vice ministers of defence and internal affairs. What help could be expected from Solomentsev, for instance, who had been promoted to Moscow from his position as second secretary to the Kazakhstan party, and with a scandal? None of them wanted to go out and talk to the people openly. More precisely, no one was capable of that because they only knew how to talk to hand-picked crowds and read prepared speeches.

An attempt was even made to get Kunayev's help, but nothing came of it. Kunayev's talk with Kolbin resulted in a decision to blame the disorder on Central Committee bureau members Nazarbayev, Kamalidenov, and Mukashev. In the heat of their ineffective anger they accused us of having stirred up the trouble and therefore held us responsible for correcting the situation. Later we learned that large forces from the ministry of internal affairs were on their way to Alma-Ata. This was their last argument, as it were. Somewhat later we were able to analyze what had happened in a more peaceful atmosphere. At the 17th Congress of the Communist Party of Kazakhstan, in both the speeches and resolutions it was stressed that the December events were not an expression of ethnic animosity, were not aimed against the Russian people or people of any other nationality. Those who wanted to see the events in that light had only one thing to say — that Kolbin was a Russian and therefore the demonstrations were anti-Russian. Clearly there was no basis to that argument. For instance, when the crowd moved from the square to the Central Committee building and demanded a discussion of who would be the new first secretary they suggested candidates such as Demidenko, Morozov and others who weren't Kazakhs but who knew the republic, its economy, traditions, and life-style. It's also understandable that many were adamant about a Kazakh taking the position. After all, out of about two dozen leaders of the republic, I am only one of three Kazakhs. The people were simply tired of leaders who came for a while and left, and looked down on all of us, whether Goloshchekin, Mirzoyan, Belyaev, Ponomarev, or Brezhnev. Later I was surprised to learn that when Gorbachev asked Kunayev who he thought should be first secretary he said it should be an outsider since none of the local leaders were worthy. I can't believe that personal animosities could be more important than the interests of one's own people. Since my name, along with many others in the Central Committee bureau, was suggested by the demonstrators as one of the possible candidates, we were kept out of the decision-making process. All the decisions were made in Kolbin's office by a small group of officials who came from Moscow. After the covert plants for forcing the demonstration to disperse were accomplished a whole series of measures were taken by the CPSU Central Committee that were supposed to improve ethnic relations in Kazakhstan. Most of them were clearly absurd. For decades the members of a hundred different nationalities had lived and worked side by side. In all my fifty years I had never, either at the factory, or in the streets, or in the stores, or in someone's home, heard any ethnic biases expressed. Never had ethnic considerations been the cause of complicated relations between people.

However, there's always a first time. I have no inclination whatsoever to seek some sinister root cause. But, unfortunately, the central government was once again undermined by its shortsightedness, its desire to do everything its own way, including the regulation of ethnic relations. Ethnic relations commissions were set up in every district centre, every town, and every village, with their own staffs. If you get a salary for doing a certain job, then you have to do it. And so the members of these new commissions went out "among the people" to ask questions, to explain who was discriminating against a German, a Ukranian, an Uighur, a Pole, a Belorussian, and how. Two young men, who were intoxicated, got in a fight at a dance over a woman. Was it absolutely necessary to determine their nationality? This is how problems were created, out of nothing. What we did essentially was provoke new conflicts and upset the historically good relations between all the many peoples of Kazakhstan.

I still don't want to go into the delicate sphere of personal relations and dwell on my attitude toward one person or another, but I can't ignore the role that Kolbin played in Kazakhstan. Clearly Kolbin was not responsible for the conflict that erupted when he came to Kazakhstan. His tragedy was that he had risen to the top in the administrative-command system, and could not give up the old methods, could not see that times had changed radically. I believe that the central government, which had drawn its mistaken conclusions about the December events of 1986, compelled him to take a harsh, dictatorial stance.

According to this style of work the main weapon of the administration is meetings. Every week a meeting was held with regional officials of all ranks throughout the party and economic system. This constant pressure resulted in all sorts of unjustifiable decisions and programs that were more declarative than anything else. For instance, promises were made that Kazakhstan's housing shortage would be solved in five years, that food shortages would be overcome as soon as possible. Sometimes the decisions were utterly absurd. For instance, one way these officials saw of carrying out the food program was to shoot wild birds and animals. All officials who did not speak Kazakh were commanded to learn the language immediately. Koblin even promised to present his report to the next Central Committee plenary meeting in Kazakh. Of course, there was the militant campaign against drinking, and the establishment of sobriety zones. As a result, problems with drug addiction grew. People even started using cologne, tooth paste and shoe polish to get high.

In my critical evaluation of such methods of administration I don't want to picture myself as an indifferent witness. Many things seemed to be quite normal and necessary. It took some time, it took making my own mistakes to see finally how useless and harmful the administrative-command system was in solving these problems. In those days my comrades in the leadership and I did all we could to support Kolbin, to help him prevent mistakes. I had no thoughts of forming anything like an opposition to the new first secretary, despite his obvious miscalculations, because we had just endured such difficult times. Kolbin took a lot of my advice on serious matters, which enabled him, as he and I believed, to get out of the dead ends. He and I had many frank conversations on this subject. This is why I was so amazed when I learned that throughout 1987 Kolbin suggested many times to the party and government leadership in Moscow that I be transferred there. Well, all I can say is that it's regrettable. Mistrust of the people you work with is a feature of the administrative-command system, and of those days when every official had to be mainly concerned with being invulnerable. It was because of the atmosphere of suspicion and secrecy, especially in the higher echelons of power. It's hard to convince people conditioned in those circumstances that you are less concerned about your career and personal welfare, and more about noble goals and interests.

That same year another blow for me was dealt by Kunayev. At the June full-scale meeting of the CPSU Central Committee when he was removed from the Central Committee and the Politburo, his last words were an accusation against me as the one to blame for all the troubles. He said that myself and others thirsting for power had caused the December events. Gorbachev interrupted him and criticized what he said. But the words had already been uttered. I was so upset that despite my good health I had to be taken to the hospital straight from the meeting.

It's no secret that the word "perestroika" has lost much of its value in recent years. It's not only because we have used the word so much in speeches, and the mass media, or because perestroika hasn't met our expectations of promoting a better life. The main reason is the society hasn't yet developed a common opinion about what the concept really means.

When it was first said out loud that we can't go on like this anymore, everyone agreed. When the policy of democratization and glasnost (openness) was declared, it also had the people's support because it was getting increasingly harder to breathe in that stifling atmosphere. At first many even thought that it was enough to promote freedom of speech and action, and that economic problems would straighten out themselves. But it soon became clear that democratization and glasnost were not so much the goal of perestroika as an important instrument that we had to learn how to use. Total confusion took over when we began making fundamental changes in the economy and government. No one really knew how to begin, what had to be discarded, what had to be saved, what had to be rebuilt. Discussions became increasingly contradictory and heated. It was hard to determine who was sincerely seeking a better way, and who was taking advantage of the political confusion just to satisfy personal ambitions. Be that as it may, a big choir of voices arose in unison out of the loud discord, demanding a fundamental cleanup that would remove the main obstacle to reforms — the Communist Party. In my opinion the formation of opposition forces to the party and the open fight for power put into the background the resolution of important social problems and as a result increased the chaos in the economy and anarchy in government structures.

I certainly don't blame the so-called destructive forces for the political and economic decline. Long ago we should have recognized that in a democratic society, which we declared as our goal, political struggle is an inevitable reality. No one is to blame but ourselves. The party was the first to state the need for decisive changes, but it could not offer society a focused and constructive reform program. We could no longer expect the rest of society to stand on the sidelines and watch the deterioration. At the very beginning of perestroika warnings were made in the party that the absence of a well-planned strategy could have unpredictable consequences. We continued to see the same flaws in the party leadership as during the period of stagnation — the total absence of self-criticism and unwillingness to listen to criticism and warnings. The party was really incapable of making serious proposals for change since it didn't have an adequate think tank. The party's major research and teaching institutions with their enormous staffs continued to serve the interests of the apparatus; they could not give up the old dogmas, so they lagged hopelessly behind modern scientific and social thought.

Let's try to put aside for a while our ideological and political differences and examine the way economic reforms proceeded in the days of perestroika. Unfortunately economic programs and the ideas expressed in the works of leading Soviet specialists on a market economy were largely borrowed from the West. As late as 1987 and 1988, virtually no one in the party was talking about transition to market relations. Only after a series of failed experiments using the method of trial and error did we begin to say there was only one solution that had worked throughout the world — a market economy. This conclusion is still the "last word" in the contemporary science of economics in this country. At first it seemed we were going in the right direction. In 1987 serious measures were elaborated to accelerate scientific and technological progress. Among these measures was stimulation of advanced innovations in production and reduction of the replacement cycles of outdated equipment, and fixed assets. An attempt was made to improve qualitatively the vitally important engineering industry. The government allocated 77 billion rubles to improve the storage and processing of agricultural produce.

Most importantly, we all recognized that the economy had to work for the people, that what the people needed was housing, food, clothing, and childcare centers, not millions of tons of steel, oil, and coal. Everywhere in the world 70 to 80 per cent of national revenues are used for consumption and the rest go for accumulation. In the Soviet Union it was just the opposite, everything was upside down. We continued building more giant factories for heavy industry, using the people's money to erect foundations, steel frames and concrete walls. The total volume of uncompleted construction reached the amount of capital invested annually into new construction. No other country in the world can boast this "distinction." This is how we used tens of billions of our petrodollars and everything else that the Soviet people produced. Finally we understood that the militarization of our economy had gone way beyond all reasonable bounds. The lion's share of national revenues went into defense industries that swallowed not only enormous material resources, but also monopolized the country's intellectual potential, its best minds and best trained engineers and workers.

We believed that after correcting these problems the economy would improve. We were encouraged by the rate of economic growth between 1986 and 1988. But hardly any changes were made to the centralized system of managing the economy. Over and over we saw the painfully familiar picture of planning, undertaking a project, then dropping it and starting another. Now even the party leadership and the government realized very well that time was running out fast. Hence the convulsive efforts to stop the imminent crisis by any means possible. One experiment after another failed. Our attempt to revive the cooperative sector was also extremely clumsy. The problems were due not only to the distortion of the idea behind the cooperative movement. One of the strongest blows was to the structure of economic relations and money circulation. This sent the whole state sector reeling. Later it was clear that conversion of military production into civilian use was no easy matter, that it required large capital investments.

The rapid growth of the national deficit forced us to give up our priority economic programmes. Chaos reigned in the economy. In these conditions the idea of the market triumphed completely. It was not however, the result of academic analysis, but the realization that this was our last hope. The sad results of the "creativity" of our economists was what forced us to embrace the ideas of a market system.

For the sake of avoiding possible misunderstandings I want to say that I was never against a market economy. The issue of concern to me is whether there is a logical and consistent way for our enormous and poorly balanced economic mechanism to be made to function with modern progressive methods of economic management, without upheavals and a lot of pain that the people would inevitably have to bear. It's hard to say if it's possible at a time when our main focus is on finding a way out of the crisis. But if we don't clarify our position now we risk the danger of making more serious mistakes.

We can't ignore the fact that the old ideas are still very much alive. From time to time attempts are made to revive methods that have already discredited themselves. In this context I would like to talk about the so-called democratization of production in the public sector. I remember well that at the June 1987 Central Committee meeting Nikolai Ryzhkov, on behalf of the government, presented a packet of documents on economic issues. One of these documents, the draft law on enterprises, stipulated that directors be elected. As a result, the heads of enterprises began playing up to their employees. They closed their eyes to violations of work discipline, and did everything they could to please one or another influential group. Many managers were so concerned with short-term interests they looked for legitimate and illegitimate ways to ensure unwarranted increases in wages, and ignored issues related to boosting labour productivity, improving quality, renewing fixed assets, and promoting social development.

Apparently someone decided that we didn't have enough public organizations at the work place and thought it necessary to establish councils of labor collectives. As a result many enterprises had dual power. Relying on the populist slogan that all workers had to be involved in managing their factory, incredible incompetence reigned in solving complex economic and management problems.

Democratization of the economy, as it was crudely interpreted, began to undermine the foundations of normal industrial operations and destabilize production relations. This is where we rejected the experience of western and world economics. This experience shows unequivocally that democratization in the sphere of material production *is* precisely the market. Everything else in this sphere is subordinate to strict discipline in every job which embraces and connects all links of the production process, the entire economic structure, including the relations between different industries and foreign economic ties. I think that in a market economy the attitudes of most of our enterprises towards filling orders would lead them to bankruptcy in a very short time.

After laying the foundation for destabilization of production from below, the central organs of government and management had no intensions of giving up their own dictate in the economy, or the petty supervision of republics, regions, and individual enterprises. Once again administrative-command ambitions prevailed over state interests and played a fatal role. Our leaders in central government thought that if they gave freedom to enterprises, and economic independence to the republics they would lose all their power. All the fundamental and vitally important problems of this country were linked to one issue, the issue of power which many people still associated with commands, directives, personal chauffeured cars, large offices with reception rooms, special telephone communications, and other prestigious elements.

The desire to keep everything as it was, despite the objective need to release the fetters on the economy, and destruction of the old relations within and between industries, increased the resistance of the republics. Furthermore, it also complicated relations between some of the republics, and added fuel to ethnic conflicts. It became unclear who owed whom what. Such misunderstandings were the result of the central government usurping the system of distribution and redistribution of sources and funds. The central government had complete control over everything produced in the republics. No one knew where their products went and in what quantity. For instance, only recently Kazakhstan learned with great difficulty who is actually getting the grain it gives the government. It turns out that it goes to all the republics. The same is true of our nonferrous metal, our vitally important raw materials and other products. The question arises, is it fair in this case to criticize Kazakhstan now for a small share of finished products in its exports (seventeen percent) and a large one (forty per cent) in its imports?

So the central government is to blame for creating the economic issues behind the many calls for sovereignty. It would be an unforgivable mistake to see this phenomenon only as political maneuvering or the result of separatist sentiments. It's another matter what forces are exploiting the side of sovereignty in different republics and in whose interests.

At the same time the desire by the republics to go off on their own has dealt a blow to horizontal economic ties, and paralyzed an enormous number of enterprises because they can't get the needed supplies from each other. However elementary common sense has led people to understand that it won't help to form isolated economic units. We've learned that even the worst economy can't survive surgical intervention. We have to find other cures. That's why after republics declare their sovereignty they naturally see the need to establish direct economic ties between themselves. The measures taken in this direction are very important. They were dictated by necessity. Experience has shown that unless our state is kept together, the various republics and peoples cannot expect normal independent development. Despite the complexities of the process of coming closer together, the prerequisites for realistically renewing the Union were created from the bottom. We finally have in our hands the tip of the thread that will help us unravel the tangled ball of political, ethnic, and economic contradictions. However, it is early to say that we are definitely on our way. So far everybody starts on the road, relying largely on themselves.

Unfortunately, the central government, which claims the role of guide, does not always have a good sense of direction. It has lost what's most important — the strategic initiative. In recent years we have seen over and over how good decisions are made, precise evaluations of one or another event are made, but all of them come after the fact. Sometimes they are several months or even years too late. For instance, at the 19th All-Union Party Conference the party and government leadership provided an accurate account of mistakes made regarding nationalities policies, but it was unable to take steps in time to prevent the dangerous development of nationalistic and separatist movements. When the party admitted (due to the pressure of the circumstances) that the sixth article of the Constitution had to be eliminated, it was unable to maintain the political initiative in the process of democratization. Promises of radical changes "within the framework of a socialist choice" that initially had the support of the vast majority of the population soon began to be called into question. No one could explain to the people what was meant by a socialist path in the new conditions, or what socialism itself was. Social scientists who had always adapted themselves to political changes, who just yesterday were persuading the people to believe that advanced revolutionary theory was flawless, were now looking for new employers. So they cheerfully launched an attack on the very ideas that, incidentally, provided them in the past with a confortable existence.

All these processes to one degree or another were happening in Kazakhstan as well and were evident in various spheres of life. Of course, someday historians, political scientists, and philosophers would be able to explain everything that happened to us and that we have yet to endure. I am offering my own opinion simply because my job kept me in the middle of events where I analyzed them, drew conclusions, and adopted decisions. It's also true that many of the difficult processes suffered by the country were not as destructive in our republic. I think that the events of December 1986 served as a good example to many. First, the upper echelons of the country's leadership began to understand that they needed to be careful in interfering on any issue, that they could make one or another problem worse. Second, people had the bitter experience of demonstrating and understood to some degree that spontaneous actions like that are not the best way to solve problems. Besides, the people sensed that there was a healthy core in the republic's leadership that was sincerely concerned about protecting their interests and the future of Kazakhstan.

Clearly not everyone appreciated this concern. Efforts continued to be made in the traditions of the administrative-command system to find enemies among the republic's leadership, nationalists and careerists. As had been the case in the past, party officials were played off one against another, according to the age-old principle "divide and rule". I remember the January 1988 Central Committee meeting in Kazakhstan when attempts were made, ostensibly to increase criticism and self-criticism, to pit one official against another, to upset relationships on a job that was hard enough anyway.

In May 1989, the 1st USSR Congress of People's Deputies confirmed Kolbin as chair of the Committee of People's Control. Consequently the first secretary of the CC of the Communist Party of Kazakhstan had to be elected. It was evident that lessons had been learned from past experience. This time opinions about the appointment were solicited from all the people's deputies in Kazakhstan, all the regional officials, and members of the intellegentsia. Ordinary citizens were questioned on the street. Only afterwards a Central Committee meeting was called to nominate me for the job of first secretary. For the first time the vote was taken by secret ballot. In June 1989 I became first secretary of the Communist Party of Kazakhstan. I think that it was at this meeting that the republic's party officials consolidated. I also had the support of those who had been pitted against me the year before. I am very grateful that this support was sincere in the conditions of totally free elections.

I took over the party's leadership in completely new conditions. The new problems that continued to arise were weighed down by the mistakes of the past. But I had neither the desire nor the time to look for someone to blame. I had to make decisions and take action.

— —

It sounds like you do not have a high opinion of Soviet economists or the well-known economic conceptions that have been discussed so heatedly in our country. Does this mean that we will have to continue solving vitally important economic problems by intuition, by empirical efforts? Since you have some hope for the Shatalin Yavlinsky program, I can't help but wonder if there is some contradiction in your position.

We cannot make progress in the economy by constant experimentation. We have already said that we've been vacillating too much in our attempts to stop the impending crisis. As a result we have only fueled the crisis with our poorly conceived measures; we have increased the potential of its strength and consequences. Now it is necessary to have a sound strategy of action, and a prognosis of how the situation will develop. Despite the confusion that continues to linger in the heads of many of our politicians and economists, and the chaos in the economy, we can see the outlines of the basis for a well planned approach. Not only the specialists generally agree that a transition to a market is inevitable, but the people as well. As late as 1988 most economists (at least those who influenced policy and shaped it), said it was impossible for the country to make this transition. But when the critical nature of subsequent developments became obvious and we began seeking ways to prevent the catastrophic collapse of the economy, we realized that the old methods wouldn't even help to partially stabilize the situation.

The Shatalin-Yavlinsky program arose in these conditions. I am critical of the program in general, and am quite skeptical of individual aspects. It is impossible to chart, practically by the day or the hour, reforms in an enormous, complex and totally imbalanced economic mechanism in a country of three hundred million. What I like about the program is its plans for stabilization aimed at improving money circulation and normalizing production relations. Although nearly everything is borrowed from world practice, it also contains elements that take into account our specific conditions and the mentality of our society. That is why I gave it my support. However the program was debated and opposed, and compromises were sought. One of the main reasons for the opposition was the fear that the people would not accept it. I don't think it's realistic to expect one hundred percent support for such radical changes. The result of all this was the Guidelines for the Transition to Market Relations. It was a symbiosis that arose more out of political considerations than basic economic interests. It was a pity. But it's naive to assume that the 500 Days was not adopted only because of political fighting. The very same Russian government that officially declared its adoption simultaneously killed the program with its own hands. I'll get back to this subject below.

One of the main reasons why we still do not have the necessary foundation for our economic changes is the government's lack of a serious think tank that could develop a program that would take into consideration both theoretical accomplishments and our own experience. It is an inexplicable paradox to me. All over the world there are special institutes dedicated to charting plans for the year ahead, five years, and even longer periods. No government takes a step without heeding these recommendations. We tend to think that people in high places are right in relying only on their own intellect and considering themselves faultless. Another problem is that although we have good theoreticians, none of them have ever lived and worked in a market economy. Theory is one thing, but you can't get practice reforming an economy by sitting in an office. That is why we have formed a group of experts in Kazakhstan and included such specialists as the American economist and businessman, Chan Young Bang, and a dean at the University of California, Los Angeles, A.S. Leijonhufvud.

In effect aren't we admitting our inability to straighten out our own house by ourselves?

I don't see anything wrong with Kazakhstan seeking the advice of western economists, and learning from others. (Incidentally, they have agreed to be paid in rubles.) Naturally it's too early to talk about the final results of these efforts, but we have already benefited from such cooperation. With the help of this group of experts we have already made some practical preparations for the partial privatization of industry and commerce, developed legal documents, signed foreign economic agreements, and created a progressive management structure. We have devised a training programme for our own personnel that would involve some western teachers, and internships in foreign companies. We will do everything possible to help these instructors understand the realities of our economy. They have already travelled widely throughout Kazakhstan studying the operation of many plants and offices. All of us are beginning to understand that it's impossible to adapt everything to our economy. Our main goal is now to carry our privatization in such a way that the employees will take over ownership, not some rich individuals with dubious backgrounds and sources of money. Soon the people of Kazakhstan will have the law on privatization. This will launch us into a qualitatively new stage of radical economic reforms.

CHAPTER EIGHT

When Others Pay for Mistakes

I don't trust politicians who frequently claim they speak on behalf of the people. These statements are often made by deputies in national and republic parliaments, regional Soviets, and representatives of various political movements. It seems that many of them tend to refer to the people when they don't have convincing arguments to back up their positions in political debates. This is when they pull out their weapons, saying the people won't understand, the people won't forgive them, the people want this and don't want that. If this doesn't work they bring out their heavy artillery and warn that the people will be the judge.

Maybe it isn't so bad when our politicians understand their responsibility to some degree and care about what people will think. But it seems to me that many of them are not very concerned about what the people will think about them tomorrow because they know the people are magnanimous, that they forgive easily, and forget big and little sins. Perhaps not everyone would agree with this observation of mine, but even at the height of the campaign exposing those who were guilty of our past calamities I didn't hear ordinary people calling for repentance or punishment.

It's no secret that the opinions of the people on many issues, including the most vital ones, are often contradictory. It's not very difficult to shape these opinions with the help of populist slogans, unscrupulous journalists and commentators in the mass media. Anyone, regardless of political preferences, can cite many examples. It doesn't hurt to examine our history in search of such examples. All we have to do is remember the tragic trials of the thirties when the people were provoked to seek out their "enemies," and gave their approval of the completely unjust and monstrous sentences. Unfortunately the majority do not always grasp the truth. This so-called opinion of the majority is often shaped by unscientific sociological studies, surveys, and even referendums. It's all in how the questions are asked.

I could dwell on this subject at length. No matter how much we try to relate the public statements and practical actions of one or another political leader to the genuine interests of the people, all the same we must admit that the main judge is the person's own conscience. Depending on his or her conscience, they either remember or forget that others, sometimes millions of others, are the first to pay for their mistakes. More often than not it is the people who have to bear the heavy burden of the consequences of hasty decisions, political and economic experiments, and sly political intrigues.

When I ask myself, "What do the people want?" I can say one thing for sure — the people want their lives to improve, and they don't want to have to wait for some distant happy future. Especially if they are told that the only way to get to this qualitatively different future is through more suffering. I don't think there is anything more irresponsible than the slogan that is so popular among a number of well-known economists—"To live better it's necessary to survive." This is a statement that can be made only by people who are convinced that because of their social status they *will* survive, and who cannot understand what it means not to have bread to feed the family, no money to buy them clothes, and no roof over their heads.

It's also important to realize that the people want to live better today, tomorrow, next week, and not in several years. If we don't promote even the smallest degree of consistent progress, then our reforms are worthless, because we already have millions of people living below the poverty line and going hungry. And a whole army of people are on the verge of losing their jobs.

That is why when I confirm my adherence to economic reforms I am convinced that we must ensure a civilized transition to a civilized market. We cannot allow the unscrupulous newly rich to make the transition crude and inhuman.

When life itself began to dictate the need for a market economy, many commentators said the people won't accept it, the people aren't psychologically prepared for the change. There were some grounds for these apprehensions. However I can't agree that our people are historically conditioned to levelling and won't accept economic inequality. What's most important is that our people won't accept dishonest wrongdoers who take advantage of them in unfair ways.

It is quite understandable why people are biased against the fat cats who have been getting rich off the shadow economy, the black market, and speculation. Hence the people fear that these types will come tomorrow to buy their plants and make them the hired help. I don't think there's any way to convince them otherwise. So there is only one way to privatize — to give only the employees the preference to buy out their enterprises. That is why I agree completely with the resolutions of the 4th Congress of People's Deputies of the USSR. They stipulate that part of the fixed assets and property of enterprises must be handed over to the employees gratis, and that the rest can be bought with the money on hand at the enterprise. Employees should also have the right to buy shares with the material incentive funds.

It should be up to the collectives alone to decide whether to sell some of the shares to outsiders, including foreigners as a way of attracting hard currency. We can move ahead significantly in our economic reforms if we explain the goals and opportunities of privatization and don't under any circumstances force these changes on the people.

I want to stress that one of the reasons why we need privatization is because our economy needs openness, without which it is impossible to have international economic cooperation. My initial experience meeting with business people from the United States, Canada, Korea, and other countries has convinced me that they are ready to conduct joint long-term programmes only if we have identical economic structures. It is not because they want to dictate their conditions and tell us what to do, which is how it was perceived in this country in the past. The problem is that there has to be mutual interest. What can a western entrepreneur gain from a Soviet manager or official who has no interest in the results of the deal because it won't change his or her salary? The employees also have no interest in such deals since it's the state that gets the hard currency under the present system. It's only natural that people have become irritated by this system because they know that the hard currency is ultimately buried in the foundations of new industrial giants.

When we start radical economic reforms we will have to ensure equal terms for all forms of ownership. Time will tell which form will prevail. Any reasonable economist knows that there is no way in the near future that all the fixed assets, and all property will go to individuals.

This does not mean, however, that the state should not interfere in any way. The state should primarily play the role of a regulator, and ensure genuine healthy pluralism in the economy. Everyone knows the consequences of the imperfections of our legislation and tax system, and the absence of a mechanism controlling incomes in the cooperative movement. Still, in Kazakhstan this did not make it necessary to curb measures that are necessary to the economy. Today 220,000 people are employed in 15,000 cooperatives of the republic. Having started essentially from scratch, by the end of 1990 they had produced goods worth 2.2 billion rubles.

Once again I repeat that a well-planned approach is needed to reform the economy. We have too many hot heads who call for going from one extreme to another. For instance, a number of economists who consider themselves agricultural experts have declared a real crusade against state and collective farms. I believe they have it all backwards. What we have to fight against in agriculture first of all are the numerous obstacles in the way of normal activities and traditional forms of working the land, and then promote new forms, including private farming. I don't think we can say today that the collective farms did not work since they were hampered from the outset by administrative yokes that stifled any initiative. After all, up until very recently these farms received not only directives on what and how much to produce, but also strict orders about where to plant, to cut, to harvest, and in what periods. It's necessary to return to the collective farms their true essence, and let them develop as genuine cooperatives, which was the original idea that was later stifled by the administrative-command system. Kazakhstan now has around 1,000 private farms, and I am convinced that they have a good future. But here again attempts are made to engage us in useless debates about whether the farmers want to take over the land or not. This is not the issue. What we have to do is give them the chance to create conditions that would enable them to get on their feet.

Farmers have to feel as though they are the true master of the land. We have been convinced of this by the results of the past three or four years. It took nothing more than simply allowing farmers to have as much livestock as they want. In this brief period the amount of cattle kept on private land increased by 500,000, and the amount of sheep and goats, by nearly two million. In 1985 Kazakhstan bought from the people no more than 30,000 to 40,000 tons of meat, but this year we estimate that the figure will go up to 130,000 tons. This has already enabled us to organize throughout the republic a whole network of special grocery stores to make food more available to the population. Unfortunately, it didn't help us when the Russian government passed a unilateral resolution in September 1990 to increase the purchasing prices of meat. This forced the national government to pass a similar resolution, since all the republics neighbouring Russia were put at a disadvantage and began losing their cattle. As a result, the national debt within the country increased by billions of rubles. Incidentally, it was from this point on that the 500 Days Programme became impossible to implement because its most stabilizing element, the most acceptable part of the plan, was undermined. The consumer was then faced with the inevitable rise in the price of meat at special grocery stores and farmers' markets.

Freeing initiative also created the basis for boosting labour productivity on Kazakhstan's state and collective farms. In the past five years, average annual farm output in the republic increased by 17 per cent, including the output of grain, by 22 per cent, meat by 27 per cent, and milk by 19 per cent. These results give me reason to maintain that we not only must, but that we *can* increase, gradually but steadily, labour productivity which is directly related to living standards.

We have been able to use capital investments realistically to satisfy the needs of the people. For instance, in 1990, 86 per cent of the republic's revenues were spent on social development. This is nearly 15 per cent more than the average indicator in the previous five-year period. As a result we were also able to make progress in other spheres of the economy. We reached the five-year targets for home building ahead of time, and the republic went from tenth place to second in the country in terms of housing availability. We built more schools, childcare centers, and polyclinics; we doubled the volume of services, and almost doubled the output of consumer goods.

However, as I mention our accomplishments I am not forgetting that store shelves remain half empty, and waiting lists for housing are nearly as long as they have always been. On the one hand I can't help but think about what serious problems we have if these fairly good indicators have hardly any impact on the people's lives. On the other hand, serious mistakes made of late have been responsible for the increasing shortage of industrial and agricultural goods. The national government's poorly conceived and coordinated statement in the middle of 1990 about raising retail prices prompted people to clean out the stores before prices went up. The people were conditioned in just a few months to stock up on all sorts of products because of other mistakes, as well as the widespread speculation and corruption in commerce. In addition, a significant part of the population has had an increase in incomes. At the same time, while incomes increased for some sections of the population, low income families fell way below the poverty line. This last circumstance makes it all the more necessary to ensure protection to low income families. Otherwise the people will not have any trust in the state, in national or republic authorities. Unless we can ensure acceptable living standards for everyone and earn the trust of the people we will inevitably drive the country to the brink of a new catastrophe. It's absurd to count on charity organizations or sporadic aid from other countries. We must not humiliate the poor, and we must not lose our own dignity.

I am convinced that the country needs a national programme to provide a safety net for the population as we make the transition to a market economy. We have to guarantee people a reasonable minimum of consumer goods and food, and clearly define the state's obligations in providing housing, medical care and other services. This should apply first of all to senior citizens, children, the disabled, large families, single parents, and other vulnerable social groups.

It is absolutely necessary to have protective measures, including the distribution of necessities in short supply. But these measures will have little effect if they are not accompanied by efforts to stabilize money circulation. The partial money reform carried out in early 1991 was necessary, but we cannot continue to depend only on palliative methods of curing the serious ills of the financial system, especially confiscation of the people's money.

The republic's program for making the transition to a market, adopted by the Kazakh Supreme Soviet, stipulates promoting privatization in the social sphere. An important factor in improving money circulation could be incentives for individual home building together with measures to privatize housing (at a nominal cost to the buyer). In 1990 alone we allocated over 90,000 farm plots to the population. However, in order for people to build private homes and country houses on a mass scale it is necessary to produce enough construction materials.

I already talked about the fact that the word perestroika was inflated in our society. Lately another concept has taken its place — stabilization. But I think that stabilization of political and economic life should not under any circumstances be associated with another round of stagnation and an end to reforms. The goal of stabilization is to prevent the further destruction of government authority and the economy. It is intended to restore basic order. Despite all the problems with excessive centralization, which I have already mentioned, we have to understand that the arbitrary destruction of the vertical structures of authority has made questionable the very existence of a unified state. The first step taken to strengthen the weak structure of government authority was the institution of the presidency, and then the formation of a cabinet of ministers. The republics have followed suit.

When the republics established presidencies they did not mechanically copy the central government. All of us remember that in the early days of perestroika many imagined that practically the main condition of democratization was a separation of legislative and executive powers. However, the gap that developed between them was largely responsible for the fact that new laws were nothing more than pieces of paper. The levers of government were lost completely.

On March 24, 1990, at a session of the Kazakh Supreme Soviet, I was elected president of the republic, by secret ballot. The election was held in accordance with the changes made to the Constitution of Kazakhstan. I do not agree at all with the opinion that the establishment of presidencies in the republics has accelerated centrifugal force, and weakened central government. First, without normal government in the republics there can be no strengthening of discipline throughout the country. Second, the way I understand the dialectics of renewal and further development of the USSR we need strong republics and a strong centre. Another issue is that of the separation of powers between the central government and the republics. Recently there has been considerable disagreement over what laws should be primary in the republics, those of the Union or those of the republics. I don't think the question should be put that way, although it follows from the contradictions between the republics and the central government that have come to the surface in the course of perestroika. I believe that the dialectics of our development are naturally reflected in these contradictions. The real danger, however, lies in the recent "war of the laws," and to some extent because of separatist forces.

It seems to me that we have found a solution. By having a Union treaty the republics can determine what powers they want to designate to the central government. In any case they will be considerable because economic relations are conducted within the framework of the union. That alone will require a centralized financial system, regulation of basic industries, coordination of foreign economic relations, and much more, without which a well-run national economic mechanism is inconceivable. The country's defence capabilities are going to be an important consideration in the foreseeable future, and will have to be managed by the central government. This division of power will determine the various functions of the national and republican laws.

In an interview for Pravda I explained in detail how Kazakhstan envisions its development in the context of its historical traditions, the specific features of its culture, economy, ethnic composition, and geographic location.

In 1989, when leaders of the Central Asian republics met in Alma Ata, some of the centre leaders perceived the gathering as threatening because some separatist game was perhaps being planned. However we had altogether different goals and expectations. Our neighbours came to the capital of Kazakhstan primarily out of concern over the crisis in the economy, a desire to work together to prevent the collapse of economic relations, and a natural inclination to survive in the following chaos. The flow of supplies between republics was becoming increasingly sporadic, and the economic crisis was deepening. For instance, in Kazakhstan our processing industries were on the verge of being closed down because the necessary raw materials were not being supplied from other republics. The situation was made even worse when we stopped getting imported raw materials for our light industry. We had to find a solution.

The agreement signed in Alma Ata between the five fraternal republics gave impetus to subsequent horizontal economic ties with Belorussia, Ukraine, and Russia. If we had any political goal at the Alma Ata summit, it was only to promote peace among the peoples of this enormous region who had lived for centuries as neighbours united by the same historical destiny.

I have already described the special features of Kazakhstan's economy. Because the republic has been exclusively used as a source of raw materials many indicators of living standards are lower than the national average. As I said, when perestroika began we were in tenth place in terms of housing availability. The republic was in sixth place in the supply of food and eighth in consumer goods. Although extracting industries were enormous, the share of processing and engineering industries in the structure of the republic's economy was half the national indicator. To this day raw materials are processed outside the republic—142 million tons of coal, 26 million tons of oil, 8–9 billion cubic meters of gas, 70 percent of raw wool and 27 percent of raw cotton.

Even so, considerable amounts of raw material resources remain unused. For instance, enormous deposits of oil and gas are still in the ground in Western Kazakhstan. We can't figure out what to do with them because we don't have capital, modern technology or equipment that would enable us to use this wealth to serve the people. At the same time we see that in other republics technology and the engineering industry are well developed. Today, however, everybody is looking toward the West for help. We could combine our efforts to establish joint inter-republic enterprises. This is being stipulated in our economic agreements with other republics. Our strategic objective is to enter the foreign market with ready-made goods.

To get off to a good start it is necessary now to attract more eastern capital, the latest foreign technology and equipment, and with their help develop our rich natural resources in a qualitatively new way, and thus make our products competitive. Like it or not, in order to live and function we will initially have to sell our raw materials and recoverable resources. Much now depends on the creation of favorable terms for a normal flow of western investments. At the same time we have to protect our economy from the damage our own businessmen can do, some of whom are ready to sell our national interest to get rich. However, no progress can be made unless our western partners see direct benefits and necessary guarantees. In accordance with the republic program for the transition to a market we have passed laws on free economic zones and free enterprise. At the same time we have created new structures enabling us to regulate the change to market economy — the Committee on State Ownership, the Anti-Monopoly Committee, the Contract Committee, etc.

Unfortunately, when we talk about a market people seem to think they know what that is, but they have only a vague idea about how to accomplish this. So far the only information we have about a market economy is from books, articles, and personal accounts. We lost a lot of time during perestroika. We could have been training our people, sending them to study abroad. During the industrialization of the thirties we sent thousands of our engineers to study at enterprises in the West. Many of them became brilliant organizers of factories, and ministers. At the same time a huge number of western specialists were invited to the Soviet Union. This historical experience gave us the idea to invite to Kazakhstan well-known economists and heads of companies who are working as consultants for the Presidential Economic Council.

It is hard to overestimate the opportunities afforded the republic by the sensible and planned conversion of defense industries. Many people associate Baikonur and Semipalatinsk with all the complex and contradictory problems typical in all aspects of our life. On one hand, these sites symbolize the great accomplishments of human thought, the outstanding results of the heroic work of millions of Soviet people, and the high level of scientific and technological progress. They instill justified faith in our people's intellectual and creative resources. On the other hand, we are faced again with a vivid example of how "higher interests" in this country go against the most basic human concerns and needs. It's enough to say that for four decades billions of rubles were invested in the space industry, but no one ever lifted a finger to improve life for the population that has been suffering from the problems of the Aral Sea. And of course not a word was mentioned about the environmental consequences of nuclear testing.

At the initiative of the public and the republic's leadership, we are promoting cooperative efforts with the research and production facilities of the space industry. Owing to our many-sided efforts we have come up with some very interesting solutions. A special programme was elaborated for the use of space technology to survey the republic's underground resources, to create new types of telephone communication, and television transmission. Specific measures have been planned to use part of the research and production complex to produce equipment for the storage and processing of agricultural goods. We are hoping to coordinate the activities of the new institute of space research to be established in Kazakhstan so that it can make the best use of our resources and help us meet our needs. A number of schools will be set up in Baikonur and a number of regional centres where young people will be able to learn about space research and technology.

I cannot possibly give a detailed picture of the goals our republic has set for this transitional period in its development, or explain all the ways in which we hope to accomplish our plans. I am simply trying to show that we have realistic prospects for overcoming the crisis phenomena in the economy, and the possibility for progress that can restore our people's confidence in the future. To succeed we need to direct all the energy in our society to constructive activities.

Recently we have heard a lot of talk about the amount of trust the people have given political leaders, new parties, and social movements. If the people have, indeed, done this it is not at all for the purpose of whipping up another political struggle just for the sake of struggle. It's time for those who have been given the trust and support of various sections of the population to stop calling others names and exacerbating political differences. We have to face the reality that the people are tired of useless political debates. It's wrong to try their patience by continually looking for someone to blame, either among the right or the left, the democrats or the conservatives, instead of genuinely seeking solutions to the problems. History has taught us that we have already been down that route, and paid dearly for our mistakes. Let's not repeat them.

Passions are high. So it's criminal to throw matches into the fire by calling for "decisive actions" outside the framework of constitutional and parliamentary methods of solving disputes and contradictions. Usually these kinds of loud statements and appeals are intended to cover up the inability to offer a concrete and creative programme of action geared to overcoming the crisis and improving people's lives. It is all the more difficult to carry out such a programme because creative undertakings require hard work on a daily basis, and not the self-admiration, demonstrations, pompous speeches, and applause that many political leaders today can't seem to live without.

We need the consolidation of society. These are not empty words. We are all united by the common goal of overcoming the crisis, promoting the people's welfare, developing the republics. Artificial obstacles to this can be created only by those who are pursuing their own, selfish interests in the political struggle. I am wary, of course, of overestimating the positive nature of the processes underway in Kazakhstan, but in my opinion the overwhelming majority of new political parties and movements seem to take this responsible position. The republic has around 100 such parties and movements, and I have spent much time with the leaders of many of them in an effort to understand their general positions, to eliminate minor differences, to develop coordinated actions and to solve vitally important problems for all the people of Kazakhstan. This kind of cooperation in the republic will promote a stable political situation, viable government structures, and work discipline, which will in turn enable us to make positive changes in the economy.

A constructive dialogue between the various political forces in the republic has enabled us to nip in the bud any efforts to whip up nationalist feelings. Our position is to promote internationalism which consolidates all sections of the population. This policy is supported by the overwhelming majority of the population representing over 100 nationalities. One of the special features of Kazakhstan is that it is the only republic in which the native population, although it is the largest group, is not the majority. This is the result of the tragic history of the Kazakh people who suffered the oppression of a totalitarian regime, and the fatal impact of the imperial ambitions of former leaders. But when perestroika enabled us to begin finally to revive the culture, traditions, and history of the Kazakhs, we realized full well that the rights and dignity of all the peoples in our republic were also stifled.

It would be wrong, of course, to say that there has been total unity around nationalities issues. The issue of language has been extremely controversial. The language of the native population was not used in government offices. Nearly thirty per cent of the Kazakh people either don't know Kazakh at all, or know it only slightly. Grandparents can't speak to their grandchildren in their native tongue. This means that the young generation is losing its roots, and doesn't know the people's intellectual traditions. However, common sense has prevailed in this issue. We were able to avoid the alienation that arose in this respect in a number of other republics. The Kazakh parliament passed a democratic law that takes into account the interests of people of all nationalities living in the republic. It stipulates measures to improve instruction in the native language of each people, and prevents any language discrimination.

The Declaration on the Sovereignty of Kazakhstan also takes into account the interests of all the peoples living in the republic. Its adoption was preceded by widespread discussion of the most important nationalities issues among all sections of the public, and a detailed analysis of all the suggestions made during this discussion. Guided by the international principle of individual human rights, the declaration ensures the equal rights of all nationalities in the republic, of all people regardless of their nationality, political and religious convictions.

Friendship between the peoples living in Kazakhstan is a distinguished accomplishment of the republic. Decades of living together and suffering together have taught all the people of Kazakhstan that different nationalities have no quarrel with each other. At the same time, each nationality, regardless of numbers or ethnic features, is great because it has behind it a fine history and rich culture contributed to by all of human civilization. Understanding this is the root of genuine ethnic dignity and healthy cultural pride. One other important circumstance has influenced the people living in this republic — Kazakhstan has always been closely connected to other parts of the country. This is not only because of economic ties that have always been strong, but because many of the people moved from other parts of the country in the past few generations. At the same time around one and a half million Kazakhs moved to other republics. Since the people have roots all over the country they feel very concerned about its future.

When we say that Kazakhstan has to find its own way to overcome difficulties, its own way of development, we are talking about the concrete methods of solving one or another economic and social problem related to the special features characteristic of our republic. We have no intentions of closing ourselves off from others, or isolating ourselves from the national problems. Life itself won't allow this to happen. We are too closely related to each other for this to happen.

Don't you feel that many foreign political leaders and statesmen are paying a great deal of attention to you as President of Kazakhstan. If so, how do you explain the interest?

I believe that the leaders of a whole number of foreign countries, firstly, are interested not only in me, and secondly, not so much in me but in the processes underway in our country. My opinion after many meetings with the representatives of other countries is that everyone wants us to have a unified state, a democratic state with an economy like that of the entire civilized world.

I want to stress that I have no ambitious aspirations when I travel abroad and meet with foreigners in the Soviet Union. What's most important to me is to justify the trust the people of Kazakhstan have in me, and to find a way to promote mutually beneficial cooperation in order to improve the people's living standards by building a market economy. I want to understand better how the economy works in other countries, and establish good contacts with the heads of leading companies. One of the results of my visits to Korea and the United States is, for instance, an invitation to well-known experts to visit our group of experts that I have already mentioned.

I was very impressed with the President of the Republic of Korea, Roh Tae Woo. Being a man of democratic convictions, he has done much to establish diplomatic ties with our country. I hope that I also contributed to the development of comprehensive contacts between our countries by telling Mikhail Gorbachev about the friendly intentions of the Koreans. One of the results of my visit to Korea was a trip to Kazakhstan by a large number of Korean businessmen who have already begun working with our enterprises. Recently Kazakhstan hosted the President of Turkey, Turgut Ozal. Here it is important to note that the people of Turkey and Kazakhstan share common historical and cultural roots and traditions. A large colony of Kazakhs live in Turkey, and they are also interested in helping to revive cultural and business ties with Kazakhstan. Of course, foreign business people are primarily interested in Kazakhstan because of the stable political situation, our rich resources, and determination to develop a market economy. In this context we are firmly convinced that cooperation should be mutually beneficial.

I have mentioned these meetings for another reason as well. The presidents of both countries, as well as the business people have confirmed that without tough discipline in productive relations it's impossible to have a market economy. I think it is necessary once again to stress this point because democracy in the economy has strict boundaries.

I could go on with the list of business contacts with western partners. My trip to the United States involved work on our country's biggest international contract. It is with Chevron to participate in refining oil in Western Kazakhstan. We discussed completing and signing the contract at confidential meetings in Moscow with US Secretary of State James Baker which were held at his initiative.

I am convinced that all these contacts and business initiatives will ultimately help our economy develop within the framework of international integration.

CHAPTER NINE

To Be Or Not To Be

The question that Shakespeare's famous hero tormented himself over is relevant to us today, and is certainly as dramatic. The answer to this question will affect the future of our country and the lives of millions of people.

History has already convinced us that to take away and divide is not the way to prosperity and social justice. It would seem that everyone has understood this truth. But apparently it isn't so. One can only wonder at how strong the desire is in some people to have a piece of the common pie, or someone else's. It doesn't even matter if the piece won't fill them up. The main thing is to feel the pie has been equally divided, "fairly."

For more than seven decades a large amount of millions of people's labor went into a common pot, and they hoped that if they contributed to the nation's wealth the state would ultimately help them overcome poverty and deprivation. Do we have the right to deceive the Soviet people who naturally long for a better life? Who has really thought seriously about what will happen if the republics go their separate ways and isolate themselves from the others? After all we can't think of our economy as a pie that can be cut into pieces. It doesn't require special theoretical knowledge to foresee the disastrous effect of cutting economic ties in such an integrated society.

It doesn't make sense to go against the flow of historical progress. If we still are unable to learn lessons from our own past, let's take another look at world history. For the vast majority of leading countries separatism has long been a thing of the past. The United States became a united country through confederation. Similar processes took place in Canada, Spain, and other countries. Today Europe is uniting and expecting big benefits from the freeing of resources that would otherwise be spend on maintaining borders, duties, patents, etc. Every state in the United States, it is true, has more independence and freedom of action than any of our republics. But this is another matter which is related to the ways in which we want to renew and structure our state.

I have discussed this issue more than once. Here I would only like to point out what I mean when I talk about the concept of a "renewed Union."

I think that most republics have made their positions clear, have reached mutual understanding on the fundamental tissues concerning the role of the central government in the system of a new state structure, the delimitations of power, citizenship, and other important aspects of urgent transformations. This coordinated platform is reflected in the draft Union treaty. Everything seems basically clear, although many details still need to be worked out. However, far from everyone approves of this clarity. Attempts are being made once again to muddy the waters by stretching the facts, raising more controversies, and generating confrontation. It is hard even for a sophisticated person to understand these political tricks. It seems to me that some people simply do not want to talk about a renewed Union and question whether there should be a Union at all.

Like the overwhelming majority in Kazakhstan, I feel this development in the discussion is unacceptable. It is regrettable that in this critical time attempts are made to distort Nazarbayev's position. Sometimes I am accused of contradicting myself by urging the preservation of the Union while criticizing the central government. I have held this position for a long time, and I don't see any contradiction in it myself. It was best summed up in my speech to the 28th Congress of the CPSU:

"As each one of us has evaluated the period of perestroika we have no doubt wondered why the party, the unquestionable initiator of social renewal, lost its leadership position; and why the CPSU has been so harshly criticized even though it has achieved important results in promoting democracy and glasnost, and fighting the Stalinist administrative-command system.

"In my opinion the main reason is because we began perestroika without a clear plan of action, without clear political and ideological directions. Today everyone is hiding behind democratic slogans like a shield — both the right and the left, including the leaders of blatant anti-socialist forces. People often don't even know whom to follow, whom to believe and support.

"How many times have we gone from one extreme to another? Two to three years ago we swore we would never consider a market economy. We were so adamantly against sovereignty of the republics, an issue that was persistently raised by communists in the Baltic republics and other parts of the country. Today we are calling for a union of sovereign states.

"Of course it is encouraging that people's thinking evolves. However, we won't go far with the method of trial and error. The party's prestige is severely undermined by decisions made in haste and then repealed. Many of today's problems could have been avoided if we had originally supported the maximum sovereignty of the republics. At any rate the central government would not be experiencing such terrible economic difficulties. How can Kazakhstan help, for instance, if ninety per cent of its industry is controlled by agencies in Moscow? Neither the Union nor the republics have anything to benefit from super centralization and monopolization.

"We have to admit honestly that after five years we cannot name any sphere in which reforms were made without significant mistakes. The only exception was in the mass media which truly made a contribution to society's renewal and did not allow the bureaucracy to squash its first shoots. But this unquestionable accomplishment also had some negative aspects. We enjoyed the euphoria of glasnost and pluralism too long; we didn't realize that these achievements were not worth much without a firm economic foundation. When the people saw their standard of living was in decline our opponents got the upper hand.

"Now the people are quite justifiably criticizing the party; they are putting tough questions to use party leaders. What can we say in response?

"I think I am expressing the opinion of many delegates when I say that the reports presented by some members of the Politburo have instilled anything but optimism. How could it be otherwise if the style of these communists in the highest ranks of the party has remained the same, and isn't in the spirit of perestroika? As before, the Politburo members had neither the time nor the desire to consult at least with the first secretaries of the parties in the republics. It's not necessary to look far for examples. Even such an important document as the framework for the country's transition to a market economy was elaborated without involving plenipotentiaries from the Union or autonomous republics. Not only party members in general, but even Central Committee members heard about this document for the first time when Nikolai Ryzhkov presented it to the USSR Supreme Soviet.

"This hasty preparation for the transition from a planned to a market economy reminds me of a desperate army in retreat. Where were our academics, whole institutes that spent decades studying the problems of market relations in the world economy?

"We are for a market economy, and primarily for the possibilities it opens up for initiative, entrepreneurship, and diverse forms of ownership. But at the same time we are for reasonable risk that has been thoroughly studied and has nothing in common with adventurism. I am deeply convinced that the idea of a market in today's circumstances goes far beyond purely economic boundaries and takes on the importance of the importance of a consolidating core. After all, an indispensable condition of genuine market relations is a unified Union of Soviet Socialist Republics, since in our country these relations can only be based on the existing unified economic complex, the existing economic ties between republics.

"We can't help but be concerned about the current situation in the country, the fact that the masses are being politicized against the background of economic decline and a weakening of administration. Flourishing barter is literally finishing off the already vulnerable system of contract commitments. We face the real danger of not reaching the targets of even this year. Unfortunately, the report by Politburo member Nikolai Ryzhkov fails to say anything about measures to prevent this from happening.

"I can't help but notice that in recent years our government has, with great persistence worthy of better application, defended the old bureaucratic structures, and leaders who adhere to the command style. It is hard to expect these people to change their methods of economic management to fit market relations.

"I believe it is possible and necessary to conclude intergovernmental agreements on economic, scientific and technological, and cultural cooperation. Recently such an agreement was signed in Alma-Ata by leaders of the republics of Central Asia and Kazkhstan, and we hope that the number of participants will increase. We are sincerely pleased by the good will shown by the new leadership of the Russian Federation, which is striving for stronger horizontal ties between the republics. We believe that such agreements will create the basis for a new Union Treaty.

"One other issue is of great concern to the communists of the republic. I am referring to the persistent efforts by some party leaders to see only the negative aspects of perestroika. Focusing on real and imaginary mistakes, they see no future for perestroika, and reject all its unquestionable accomplishments. They want the people to believe that perestroika is the root of all evil. Is this out of confusion, nostalgia for the days of stagnation, fear of the party rank and file, or everything together?

"Undoubtedly the route of renewal has been much more complicated and treacherous than we suspected in the beginning. But in the past five years we have learned something about democratic reforms. We must give credit to the people who have literally suffered the hard experience of leading the country into these new and unusual conditions. Besides, it is time for us to finally learn to respect our own country and the leaders that we elect. Here I feel it is my duty to tell you the opinion of the delegates of the 17th Congress of the Communist Party of Kazakhstan. They unanimously supported nominating Mikhail Gorbachev for the post of General Secretary of the CC CPSU.

"An analysis of various programs and platforms shows that we have many more points of view in common than in opposition. All of us are for improved living standards, for a strong and prestigious country on the world scene. Political compromise is absolutely necessary today, and the only way to achieve all these goals. We have no other choice."

It is hard to find contradictions between the problems I raised at the party congress and the fundamental positions that I expressed at the 4th Congress of People's Deputies of the USSR. But the central government reacted very negatively to my latter speech. Some people even accused me of seeking confrontation. Well, if anyone thinks it's possible to consolidate by accommodating those phenomena that have been long intolerable and slowed down our country's development, then we truly have different paths to follow. We know only too well the price of "unity" under the administrative-command dictate. I think the only way we can unite is if we first solve what divides us.

Incidentally, my position is stated fully in this speech, and so I will cite it here as well:

"I would like once again to use a metaphor that our parliamentary correspondents like so much. Yes, for the fourth time we have gathered in our large and slow ship. If before our political sea was only somewhat wavy, now it is stormy. It is very turbulent, and the helmsman is vacillating. Is it any surprise that part of the crew wants to take over the helm, change the course, while a second group wants to get the lifeboats ready in hopes of continuing the trip separately, and a third group wants to return to the shore that we left not so long ago? The stir among former Brezhnev's comrades-in-arms testifies to that.

"Naturally it is only an illusion that the administrative-command system we have been fighting for six years has been crushed. Nothing of the kind. The dictatorial habits of the central apparatus have not weakened. The declarations of sovereignty by the republics have not shaken the monopoly positions of the ministries who could not care less about our sovereignty. Foreign economic relations are still in their hands, and our attempts to earn hard currency are still impeded by the presidential decrees that were prepared by the government and are blocking objective economic laws. Where will you find such a naive altruist who would agree to legal theft and give to the government 95 per cent of the hard currency he earns? We surely suffered a defeat when we didn't adopt a program to switch to a market economy, but instead replaced a clear plan with non-committal Fundamental Guidelines.

"The recent actions of the USSR Council of Ministers were essentially geared to destroy our country's unified economic space. I am talking about the introduction of fixed wholesale prices on raw material resources, the hike in purchasing prices on farm produce, and the new tax regulations. The problem is not only that all these actions are seriously damaging the economies of the republics. What's much worse is that the government is letting retail prices be decided locally. This is clearly being done because all the "games" with prices are extremely unpopular among the people. Therefore the government wants to make the republics bear the responsibility. But if Uzbekistan has one price, Kazakhstan another, and Russia still another, it will cause terrible speculation throughout the country, and the people will carry an additional burden.

"It's time to say quite frankly that the mistakes made in conducting the economic reforms have brought the country to the threshold of a crisis unprecedented in our history.

"We value the diplomatic talent of our president. But it seems as though his intensive use of these abilities to the detriment of decisive action is beginning to have bitter results. The artificial reanimation of the stillborn government programme for the transition to a market economy, undertaken for the sake of maintaining the government's prestige, is certainly not a compromise that should be applauded. We have made a match between two antipodes and are now waiting for the monster that will be born as a result of this unnatural marriage.

"Political rope-walkers are turning our movement towards a market economy into a bluff. Our country is borrowing billions without any guarantee that they will be used right. We are entering a market without properly trained people who know market relations down to the last detail. Not even a totalitarian system could afford such irresponsibility in the economy. On the eve of industrialization hundreds of Soviet engineers were sent to western countries to study, and just as many foreign specialists worked in our industries. It is hardly surprising, therefore, that Soviet entrepreneurship is extremely vulgarized, that it is geared to make money fast and not to build long-term business prospects.

"For the sake of clarity I'd like to stress that in strategic terms I agree with the policy of Mikhail Gorbachev and take a strong stand on this. However, the policy of perestroika demands, in my opinion, a change in tactics within the country and decisive actions in the most important areas.

"I can't agree with the policy by which our country, after choking on the sweet syrup of high-sounding words about democracy, has gone looking for bread off the wealthy tables of Europe. The humiliated and offended people have the right to ask you, Mikhail Gorbachev, and you, Nikolai Ryzhkov, where are the fruits of the promised modernization in our engineering industry and the widely advertised economic conversion? Where are the concrete results of the programme for scientific and technological progress that was announced so long ago? Where are the 77 billion rubles allocated to develop the processing of farm produce? These practical steps, from which we started perestroika, were right decisions, but the good intentions were lost in political rhetoric. Today our best engineers and most skilled workers in the defense industry are producing ordinary frying pans. I don't suppose I'll be giving away any state secrets if I say that the KGB organized an exhibit of ordinary consumer goods manufactured in the West. Thank you comrades, the exhibit is truly interesting. But if this is what the state security system is doing, then why do we need a Council of Ministers? It's shameful and painful to have to talk about all this.

"In this context I'd like to ask you a direct question. Are we going to continue much longer with this useless criticism of our mistakes? We have to get an answer to these questions. If prices are increased, will some compensation be made? What is the budget of the Union and republics for 1991? Will we switch to a market economy? We don't have an answer yet. If we entrust this transition to the current government the whole effort will fail because building market relations goes against all its objectives. That's why I am urging you to make a decisive step, to return to the logic and framework of the Shatalin-Yavlinsky programme, and adopt it, of course with some amendments, as a plan that can help us out of the crisis. Incidentally, Yavlinsky's resignation should be regarded as a desperate attempt to call attention to the fact that our government will not listen at all.

"Recently we have heard many sarcastic remarks about the so-called 'parade of sovereignty.' Yes, there has been a 'parade,' but it's a big mistake to interpret it only as motivated by local, ambitious interests, and not see the profound reasons for this process. The reasons are due to the paralysis of the central government, the egoism of national ministries and agencies that will never agree to give up their dictatorial privileges. Hence, the collapse of the economy, the increase in crime, and the whole host of inter-ethnic conflicts. Should we throw stones at the republics which are simply trying to somehow protect themselves from the destabilizing policy of the central government? Can they be accused of separatism only because they are expressing the normal desire for self-preservation in the impending chaos?

"Furthermore, having grown accustomed all these decades to the central government organizing everything, we missed the time when declarations about sovereignty could have the maximum effect, could stop the overwhelming process of the destruction of horizontal ties. Today the republics can no longer wait. They are acting on their own, and are taking responsibility themselves for the Union. Political and economic independence is the only way each republic can develop separately and together with all the others.

"I am not inclined to panic when I hear that our Union is collapsing. No am I inclined to blame the central government too much. Do you know why? Because sooner or later it is inevitable. A building with a bad foundation will not stand for long. We saw that when the first wind of common sense blew in April 1985. The basically sound Leninist plan for our common home had not been properly implemented. After all, the republics did not united around the central government, but the central government attached the republics to itself. So now we're seeing the inevitable process of collapse. At the same time a new Union is arising, one of the better developments in our otherwise disturbing situation. I am referring to the signing of treaties between republics in which each other's sovereignty is recognized, current borders are confirmed, and direct economic ties and coordinated interests are established. I am certain that these documents form the basis for a new Union treaty, and foundation and structures of our renewed federation that Kazakhstan supports.

"Some people claim that the republics are challenging the central government with their bilateral and multilateral treaties. This is essentially true, but what we are challenging is the totalitarian central government and its administrative-command system that has suppressed all initiative and brought the country to a dead end. The only way out of the dead end is to go back. That is why the principle that we followed blindly for so many decades has to be read from the other direction, and then everything will work well. It is not the central government that should determine how the republics live, but the republics that should say what the central government should be like and what powers it should have.

"We will have to work out the details of the Union treaty together. But during the debates, at all times in this process, let's not forget the main goal. And that is the decisive renewal of our multi-ethnic country — the Union of Sovereign States — toward the integration, spiritual unity, political and socio-economic consolidation of our peoples."

Perhaps the criticism I expressed against the country's leadership at the party congress, the latest USSR Congress of People's Deputies, and in a number of interviews in the mass media might seem to some to be too harsh. But I consider my criticism to be well-founded, logical, and consistent. The national government should not conduct its basically sound strategic policy with methods that impede perestroika in general, and prevent the republics from getting out from under the humiliating detailed guardianship of the central government, with its desire to regulate every step they take and curb their creative initiative. After all, central bodies are still interfering in the affairs of individual enterprises. I am certain that in these conditions any healthy criticism is useful and without it we won't move ahead. I think that criticism has significantly helped us progress in a number of vitally important issues. Perhaps not as quickly as we would like, but we are still managing to overcome resistance to the fundamental principles of renewal of the Soviet Union as the Union of Sovereign States and that were proposed by most republics and coordinated by them.

At the same time I firmly support all sincere efforts by the national leadership to consolidate our society. I cannot understand the unjustified attacks on their reasonable actions. Sometimes opposition is expressed the moment they do anything to improve the situation only because the actions are being taken by the central government. We can't build serious political relations by being against everything just for the sake of protesting. This has already resulted in an uncoordinated programme of action throughout the country. We are forced to resolve crucial national problems without any time for proper consideration. I don't want to start pointing fingers at who is most to blame.

If some republics don't want to be in the renewed Union we can't force them. But I don't think that we can deceive ourselves indefinitely and give people the illusion that they can get to a better life on their own. The core of a future new state, including those republics involved in drafting the Union treaty, has already been formed. The foundation of its strength is the powerful economic potential accounting for at least 80 per cent of what the fifteen republics together represent today. Therefore it is not necessary to force anyone into the Union. Let them think it over; time will help them make their choice.

This is just one aspect of the problem based only on the hard, cold reality of economics. Those who are turning away from the Union today should keep in mind that there are millions of people who don't want to live outside their own country. At any rate, I have difficulty imagining how it's possible to cut the ties that bind the 70 million people who live outside their native republics, and the millions of families that have resulted from mixed marriages. We can't condemn people for their sacred feeling that they belong to one great country. What can be done if this sentiment is stronger than the political ambitions of separatists? It would be better if we don't wait for the results of the new experiments, and once again seriously think about the possible consequences. Not so long ago the Supreme Soviet of Kazakhstan expressed its firm stance and determination to preserve our country as the renewed commonwealth of sovereign states. I think that the Appeal to all Supreme Soviets of the Republics in the USSR, unanimously adopted by Kazakhstan's people's deputies, reflected the aspirations not only of the overwhelming majority of the people of Kazakhstan, but of every Soviet person who is not indifferent to our common destiny. I also hope that this document will be accepted by those who still have not made a final decision.

Appeal by the Supreme Soviet of Kazakhstan to the Supreme Soviets of the Republics of the USSR:

"We, the people's deputies of the Kazakh Soviet Socialist Republic, expressing the anxiety and aspiration of the peoples in our multi-ethnic republic, guided by concern for the vital interests of millions of our voters, the voice of our own common sense and conscience, in this critical time for the future of our country, appeal to the Supreme Soviets of all fraternal republics of the USSR to demonstrate political wisdom, constraint, and foresight, and to do everything possible to prevent a catastrophe, the collapse of our great Union.

We cannot close our eyes to the reality of such a tragic development at a time when destructive forces, on behalf of personal and group ambitions and narrow selfish interests, are exploiting the idea of free national development of peoples, and are undermining the inter-ethnic friendship that was sealed with blood and sweat.

Unquestionably, we have serious reasons in our history for mutual resentment, disappointments, and doubts. They are the result of decades of domination by the administrative-command system, which usurped power in our common home and the right to speak and act on behalf of the peoples. We can shake off the totalitarian past only by working together and uniting our efforts.

The Kazakh people, all the peoples of the republic, cannot conceive of themselves outside our united country whose preservation is in the political and economic interests of multi-ethnic Kazakhstan. The collapse of the Union will inevitably bring about the complete destruction of the economies of the republics, drastically undermine the lives of millions of people, set us back whole decades, and irreversibly damage cooperation with countries in the world community. We have no alternative but to renew the Union by concluding a Union treaty between sovereign and equal republics.

We firmly adhere to this position but also clearly realize that it is impossible to build a new federation while rejecting healthy national foundations and ignoring constitutional government acting in accordance with the will of all the Soviet people. It is dangerous to turn contradictions between the republics and central government (that are only natural in the process of perestroika), into a 'war of laws' that can cause unpredictable civil confrontations. It is all the more dangerous to try and create a 'parallel central government' because it would inevitably destabilize the political situation in the country.

It is necessary to build a strong obstacle to destructive centrifugal forces. We believe that the people's deputies of the Russian Federation have a special mission in this respect, since the peoples of Russia, that have experienced the full impact of the administrative-command system, can and should play an important, constructive role in shaping a renewed Union.

The aggravated political situation will not allow us to wait until all the republics decide whether they want to sign the Union treaty. It is necessary to immediately begin a dialogue with those who are for preserving the country's unity and reserve for the rest of the republics the right to join any time when they make their final choice. Relying on the adopted declarations on state sovereignty, we are obligated to give clear answers to fundamental questions, such as, what will our Union be and what will our new central government be. This is especially important now when it is clear that the central ministries and agencies are trying to ignore the sovereign rights of the republics.

The people of Kazakhstan, who defended Moscow in the harsh year of 1941, provided the country with bread, made available the launch pad that took us into Space, care very much about the future of the country. We are for the strong unity of sovereign republics, further strengthening of the democratization and humanization of society, that will ensure political, social, economic freedoms and guarantees to every person regardless of nationality. We want to join together with all the other republics of our multi-ethnic country in a renewed Union."

The Appeal of the Supreme Soviet of Kazakhstan to the Supreme Soviets of all republics of the USSR, the constructive participation in the elaboration of a Union treaty and a number of other measures taken by the republic's leadership are evidence of Kazakhstan's important consolidating role in cementing the Union. I would like to better understand your vision of a renewed Union. Would this be a Union of sovereign states or sovereign republics, a confederation or a federation? After all, many serious contradictions are caused by contradictory interpretations of the thin line drawn between these two concepts.

The aspiration for the renewal and preservation of a strong Union is not simply the policy of the leadership of the republic. It is the strong will of all peoples in multi-ethnic Kazakhstan expressed in the results of the recent referendum. Over 94 per cent of those who voted said "yes" to our Union. Incidentally, the number of people who voted in the referendum was the highest in recent years. Not even that many people came out to vote for people's deputies of the USSR, or the Supreme and local Soviets in the republic. Now about prospects for the future. I don't think we should get bogged down in debating how a sovereign republic differs from a sovereign state. Article 76 of the current Constitution of the USSR clearly states that a Union republic is a sovereign Soviet socialist state that together with the other Soviet republics is united in the Union of Soviet Socialist Republics. This was the basic principle we followed when we adopted the Declaration on Sovereignty. No one invented anything new. It's another matter that the concept in this country of a "sovereign state" has lost its meaning in reality. The resurrection of genuine state sovereignty of the republics is the basis for the renewal of the Union. This does not mean, however, that our republics cannot have federative relations. It's not possible to have absolute independence if we're talking about an indivisible economic territory, and the need to preserve a single army for the sake of common security. What's more, the further integration of the economy, in my opinion, will inevitably lead to closer unity of the republics, and will help overcome the elements of alienation that have developed in recent years.

You have thoroughly analyzed the reasons for our current sad situation, and have mentioned the measures that are being taken in the republic to overcome, or at least lessen, the impact of the crisis phenomena. Any sober-minded person would agree with your conviction that it's impossible to expect a good future without the preservation and renewal of a national state. But preservation of the country's unity, a strengthening of the republics' independence, and transition to a market economy are only individual, although important, conditions toward a well-coordinated program of action. The people are tired of improvisation that sometimes merely increases the contradictions. Do you have any vision of such a programme?

I think that our strategic direction should be to create market relations in the economy. Today the crucial issue is to ensure consistency, and coordinated actions to strengthen the vertical ties of the Union and horizontal inter-republic relations. It's necessary to be realistic. By no means all the potential of the crisis has come to the surface. If we continue to act separately from one another and increase political confrontation the extent of the damage will be tragic. In order to take control of the situation it is necessary, in my opinion, to do the following:

First, we all have to understand that what's most important today is to emerge from the crisis in the economy and give people faith in the future. For this to happen the government will have to come up with a clear programme of action to stabilize the economy and make a transition to market relations. The government will need a mandate of trust and power for a certain period and take full responsibility for the results.

Second, for two to three years we will have to extricate the economy from ethnic and inter-ethnic problems. Only the early conclusion of a Union treaty will make this possible. I am certain that, with rare exceptions, there are no irreconcilable differences or confrontations between the republics or between peoples. But since these problems continue to come up, it's hard to expect total national accord in the near future. Therefore it is necessary through joint efforts to develop ways to exclude the disintegrating and destructive impact of these problems on the economy. The possibility and efficiency of these measures are confirmed by the conclusion between republics of horizontal economic agreements. Such principles must become the foundation of relations between the republics and the central government.

Third, it is necessary clearly to understand that we no longer have a single ideology that for many years was a strong uniting factor. Therefore any attempts by political forces to take the lead no matter what are unwise. It is also useless to appeal for consolidation. But political compromise is necessary. It will enable us to prevent the erosion of economic ties which will be disastrous for everyone.

Just a few more unreasonable decisions and the situation will become irreversibly hazardous in every respect. Therefore it is necessary to enact special decisions limiting for a designated period any actions that disrupt coordination in the economy. It is not a matter of choice. We have no alternative.

At the same time we cannot permit steps that prevent the development of democratization. But democracy has nothing in common with anarchy, license, and unconstitutional actions. In order to make real progress it is time to make the transition from glasnost to free speech, from demonstrations to parliamentary methods of struggle, from sweeping criticism to the proposal of concrete political and economic programmes.

I am a consistent advocate of creating equal material conditions for the development of all constitutional parties and movements, and of open competitive struggle for influence and power. But in the economy we need clarity. People have to follow the law, have to be disciplined, and exhibit a sense of responsibility. Without this it is simply impossible to make the transition to a market economy. All parties and movements can engage in political struggle, but if we are to stabilize the economy and build new market relations we have to forbid any kind of partisan or ideological interference in this process.

In conclusion I would like to stress once again that we can't afford politics that put personal ambitions first, and that monopolize the right to truth. In my opinion the desire for self-preservation should tell us that any action increasing economic and social chaos will result in a storm that will blow us all away. The whole political superstructure will come down at once, together with its "centre," the "right" and the "left." Remaining in the rubble will be not only those who created the failed programmes, but also the people's last hopes for a normal life. This outcome is quite possible. It can be prevented only by the policy of common sense.

Don't you think we're ending the book on a pessimistic note?

I would call it a realistic note. After all, we won't be able to avoid many difficulties, such as the further decline in output with all the attending consequences. But I think we can survive all these troubles and not hurt the people who trust us.

Epilogue

Events have made it necessary to add this epilogue to a book which has already been written. History has passed its final and irrevocable verdict on those who attempted to reverse its course, those who tried once again to subordinate the logic of the objective laws of social development to crude, neo-Bolshevik political gangsterism.

There are those who are inclined to see the failure of the August putsch as proof of the conspirational incompetence of its organizers, who are presented as timid, hesitant amateurs. Even Brezhnev, they argue, needed only one day to "overturn" Khrushchev, despite the fact that in 1964 the situation in the country was far less tense, and therefore, less favourable for a coup. At first glance it might indeed seem so. However, I am deeply convinced that one cannot use historical analogies outside their particular context. In contrast to October 1964, when the population was silent, a mere observer of the battle for power, in August 1991 that population was no longer prepared to accept the passive role which had been assigned to it. The humiliating paralysis of inbuilt fear which had held more than one generation of Soviet citizens in its grip, forcing them to accept whatever political and ideological postulates were handed down "from above" as inevitable and beyond doubt, this time proved unable to hold down a society recovering its health. Six years of painful perestroika, albeit not always consistent, and at times even contradictory, had nonetheless not been in vain. The people had savored their first breath of freedom, and this proved sufficient for them to shake off the bonds of blind obedience, and once and, let us hope, for all time, reject any return to an anti-democratic, totalitarian regime.

One can issue orders to those who are prepared to obey, those who are morally broken and deceived. This is precisely what made the repressions of the 1930s and 1940s possible. I do not think that Yanayev, Kriuchkov, Pugo and others of their kind would have hesitated in certain circumstances to use the methods of Yezhov or Beria. However, the fact of the matter is that today these new "fathers of the nation" were facing a different country and different people, and they cannot have failed to realize it. That explains their "wait and see" tactic, their attempts to win over the republics, their fear of radical measures which, had the political situation been different, they would not have hesitated to implement. Nonetheless, the Yanayev group relied above all on the element of surprise in the hope that force, backed up by the army, the KGB and the Ministry of Internal Affairs, would paralyze opposition to their dictatorship.

In my case it all began with an unexpected telephone call to my office from Moscow on the morning of August 19, immediately after the radio had broadcast the news of the creation of a State Emergency Committee. At the other end of the line was Yanayev, who was clearly anxious to hear my reaction to this devastating piece of news. My first question was about Gorbachev: where was he? what had happened to him? The reply was reassuring: Mikhail Gorbachev was still in the Crimea, but was informed of what was happening, and agreed that "order had to be restored in the country." Not believing my ears, I repeated my question, and was told once again that Gorbachev was informed about the actions being taken by the Emergency Committee, and had given them his approval.

I had never had a high opinion of Yanayev, but I had never imagined that he was capable of such bare-faced deceit, and so for the first few minutes I was in a state of shock. It was, after all, only two days since my last conversation with Gorbachev, during which we had discussed in detail a whole range of issues relating to the new Union treaty. I knew very well how the President of the USSR viewed this political document. I myself had witnessed the enormous efforts he had made to ensure that the treaty would finally be signed. And now, when the goal was nearly reached, an abrupt change of policy? It all seemed very suspicious. My doubts were further increased when Yanayev was unable to give me a clear answer to my question as to where exactly the state of emergency was to be introduced. The vague statement that a state of emergency would be introduced "in certain regions of the country" in fact allowed the Committee to blackmail any republic, region or city. I realized that all my dark forebodings prompted by the increasingly unstable situation in the country over the previous months had come nightmarishly true.

Yet it had seemed that the worst lay behind us. I had returned only a few days previously from Tashkent, where we had held the second meeting of the republican leaders of Central Asia and Kazakhstan. We had all agreed that the new Union treaty would provide an acceptable basis for redistributing power between the central government and the republics, opening up broad perspectives for republican sovereignty in both the political and economic spheres. In particular it was emphasized that the country could overcome the crisis in which it found itself, only by the united efforts of all the republics; that economic and social recovery was inseparably linked to stability, discipline and order, and required the elimination of ethnic and civil strife. A special communique along these lines was drawn up and signed by all the republican presidents.

On August 16 I returned in good spirits to Alma-Ata, where I had another important meeting—this time with Boris Yeltsin. The purpose of his visit was the ratification of a bilateral agreement on friendship and cooperation between Russia and Kazakhstan. I realized, however, that the reason for this visit was something far more important than the simple exchange of signed documents. A conversation with the Russian leader on the eve of the signing of the Union treaty is not merely a routine "protocol" meeting, all the more so as Boris Yeltsin, a striking figure on the political scene, is a man always calling for the most decisive reforms and radical changes. Openly proclaiming economic and political principles which only yesterday were wholly unacceptable for the totalitarian-socialist system, he had overcome the resistance of the party-state machine and achieved the apparently impossible — he had become President of Russia. Each new stage in his political biography represented the fracture and disintegration of social and political dogma.

In short, I saw this meeting as very significant. So it turned out to be. As a result of this visit to Kazakhstan by a state delegation of the Russian Federation, a number of important documents were signed. Yeltsin and I signed joint agreements, "On Guarantees of Stability in the Union of Sovereign States," and "On a Single Economic Territory." The chairman of the Russian Council of Ministers and the Prime Minister of Kazakhstan signed an agreement on the principles of trade and economic cooperation between the Russian Federation and Kazakhstan for the year 1992.

It was also during this visit that Yeltsin and I formulated the idea of participating directly in efforts to resolve the Armenian-Azerbaijan conflict. We were both firmly of the opinion that an end must be put to this bloody and shameful battle within a community of civilized nations. Ethnic problems cannot be resolved by the use of force. Such methods have always and everywhere led only to escalation of the conflict, to more bloodshed and the mass violation of human rights. Since the opportunity to resolve the conflict earlier had been lost as a result of mistakes by the Union government, we decided that the leaders of sovereign republics should take steps genuinely aimed at securing peace. We proposed that energetic measures be taken to arrange immediately for direct negotiations between the leaders of the two opposing sides, including respected leaders of the Armenian population in Azerbaijan, the Azerbaijan population in Armenia, and all forces capable of influencing the situation in the region. We also decided not to set any preconditions, and to act, if this was acceptable to both sides, as intermediaries in the negotiations and guarantors of any decisions taken. We set out our proposals in a detailed letter to the President of the USSR and the leaders of Armenia and Azerbaijan.

Thus Yeltsin's visit to Kazakhstan culminated in the signing of a whole series of important documents designed to ensure the most favourable conditions for the Union treaty.

There was, of course, also the unofficial side of this visit. I found it very interesting to talk to a man whose career had been full of dramatic surprises, who had lived through moments of defeat and moments of triumph. Yeltsin is a fairly good tennis player (and also a Master of Sport in volleyball, a sport which I myself also like), and so during his visit to Alma-Ata we at last managed to spend a couple of hours on the tennis court. A match of this kind tends to reveal a man's true character, and the match had only just begun when I realized that I was dealing with a rather stubborn and proud man who found defeat painful to accept. He lost two fingers as a teenager, and this affected his backhand, a fact which I made allowances for, and this, it seems to me, he appreciated. Our match ended in a draw, and when we left the court our ties of friendship had been strengthened.

On the last day of Yeltsin's visit I suggested that he visit the district where I was born and grew up, only a few dozen kilometers from Alma-Ata and immensely picturesque. The snowy peaks of Ala-Tau, the wonderful mountain air, the white yurtas (nomad tents) pitched along the banks of a mountain stream and, it must also be stated, the unique Kazakh cuisine, left a powerful impression on him. The relaxed, informal atmosphere favoured frank discussion of many important issues, and I became more and more convinced that my personal friendship with Yeltsin constituted an important factor in ensuring fruitful relations between Russia and Kazakhstan, and in promoting those major political and economic changes which we agreed to carry through together in the future.

Both of us enjoyed the meeting, and time passed unnoticed. The only "incident" was when Yeltsin repeatedly expressed his desire to take a swim in the stream. Such a desire was quite understandable if one bears in mind that for someone from Russia the weather was unusually hot. However the water in the stream flowed directly down from the mountains and was icy cold. To bathe in it could have unpleasant consequences. Therefore, although Kazakh tradition means that the wish of a guest is law for the host, I permitted myself on this occasion to violate custom. "Over my dead body," so to speak. My final argument was to remind him of the Union treaty, which was to be signed in two days' time. All we need, I argued, is that on that potentially historic day the Russian leader should be in bed with pneumonia. Your own Russian citizens would never forgive either of us. In the end, albeit with difficulty, I dissuaded him.

Yeltsin had agreed that his departure from Alma-Ata be delayed for three hours. As it later turned out, this proved to be a major factor in later events. After the putsch, Yeltsin discovered that the security forces under Kriuchkov had been planning a terrorist attack on his plane as it returned from Alma-Ata, and this delay disrupted all their plans.

Let us return, however, to the events of August 19. The next telephone call was from Kriuchkov, chairman of the KGB. He informed me in a condescending, not to say haughty tone that the powers of the central authority had been transferred to the Emergency Committee, giving me to understand by his very manner that any discussion of the lawfulness of actions taken by this Committee were quite out of place. To my question as to the fate of Gorbachev, and his reaction to this turn in events, Kriuchkov replied that the President of the USSR was in a critical state of health, quite incapable of governing the state, and had agreed to the transfer of power. This transfer would be, so he informed me, formally legalized within a few hours.

I immediately contacted Lukyanov, chairman of the USSR Supreme Soviet. However, he was unable to tell me anything definite, pointing out that he had himself only just returned from holiday, and was not in possession of all the facts.

My next conversation was with Prime Minister Pavlov. Unlike Kriuchkov, Pavlov attempted to conduct the conversation in a friendly, confidential tone, to "sugar the pill." He began by stating that the government of the USSR would continue the policy of radical economic reforms, and then shifted to the critical condition of the national economy, expressing the view that it was at the edge of the abyss, that the harvest was not being collected, that there was sabotage everywhere — in short, extraordinary measures were needed to overcome the crisis, and that this was not a time for constitutional niceties.

These conversations took up the entire morning. At two in the afternoon I called an extraordinary meeting of the Presidium of the Supreme Soviet and the Cabinet of Ministers of Kazakhstan and passed on to them what little information I possessed. The opinions expressed varied. Some were clearly afraid. Others, not yet grasping the implications, fell back on reserved acceptance of "orders from above," and were ready to give unquestioning support to the Committee. The majority, however, were in favor of adopting a political position independent of orders from the new "Soviet government".

As President of a sovereign republic, I was concerned above all to preserve stability in Kazakhstan. I saw my main task as being to protect the people of Kazakhstan against any social upheavals in a tense situation fraught with unpredictable consequences, and to prevent any ethnic or other conflicts which might serve as a pretext for bringing in troops. Such a danger could not be excluded.

I proposed the immediate publication of an address to the people of Kazakhstan. Here is the full text of this address as broadcast on television and radio on August 19, 1991.

> "People of Kazakhstan!
>
> After consultation with the members of the Presidium of the republican Supreme Soviet and Cabinet of Ministers, I am making the following appeal.
>
> At an hour so critical for the country, I call upon you to maintain calm and show restraint. This is *especially necessary* now, since any emotional, ill-considered action by any one of us may become the spark that sets off serious upheavals.
>
> I appeal to all citizens, to all nationalities and ethnic groups living in our multi-ethnic republic. At such a moment we must rely on that centuries-old multi-national harmony which has always been for us the basis of our unity and mutual understanding.
>
> I appeal to the workers of Kazakhstan. At such a time *it is very important* to maintain a high level of responsibility and organization. We must not allow the economy to slide into chaos. Rural workers bear a special responsibility, since the fate of the harvest and food supplies is in their hands.
>
> I appeal to all political forces and organizations in the republic. We must put aside tactical differences, adopt a rational and responsible position and not allow confrontation to develop.
>
> I appeal to those serving with the Armed Forces and in units of the KGB and Ministry of Internal Affairs stationed on the territory of Kazakhstan to adhere to constitutional norms, to respect the rights of the individual and the local authorities. I

would like in particular to stress the fact that a state of emergency is not being introduced in Kazakhstan and that, in accord with the adopted Declaration on state sovereignty and the Constitution of the Kazakh SSR, all authority lies with the Soviets.

I repeat my support for the policy of strengthening the sovereignty of the republics, for the principles of democracy and the preservation of the Union. I am resolved to carry through the reforms already begun, and I am firmly convinced that the people of Kazakhstan will display responsibility, alertness and unity."

That same day, August 19, Yanayev telephoned again. It would seem he was disturbed by the active resistance shown by the Russian leadership and by increasing tension in Moscow, and wanted to secure our support. He even resorted to direct deception, assuring me that other republics had accepted the Committee. I told Yanayev outright that the assumption of the role of head of state and the creation of the Emergency Committee were, in my opinion, unconstitutional acts, and asked him what he himself thought of the legal aspect of his actions, and whether he had considered the fact that he acted in violation of the Constitution of the USSR. This self-appointed "savior of the fatherland" replied with cynical frankness that he fully appreciated all of this, but that politics was not about keeping your hands clean, and any methods were acceptable that would achieve the purpose. Later the Supreme Soviet would find a way to legalize the new power.

Following this conversation I had no more doubts as to the actual intents and purposes of the Committee, and I immediately began to draft a Statement expressing my political assessment of events. I believed it necessary to emphasize in this Statement that the Emergency Committee was issuing manifestly unlawful documents which, amongst other things, encroached on republican declarations of sovereignty and disregarded the policy of moving to a market economy. "If we continue along the crooked path of lawlessness," I wrote, "the people will not forgive us. Above all, in these difficult days, we wish to hear the opinion of Mikhail Gorbachev himself. He must personally confirm his incapacity to perform the duties laid upon him."

I read out this Statement on republican television and radio on August 20. That same day my press service sent a video recording to central television. Thus Kazakhstan was the second republic after Russia to express sharp condemnation of the putsch. On August 21 we were joined by

Kirghizia. The Committee was not slow to react. As soon as my Statement had been broadcast in Kazakhstan, telephone calls from Moscow ceased, and central television was told that under no circumstances was the video recording to be broadcast. However, it was impossible to force us into silence. The press service managed to give the text of the Statement to various mass media, including some overseas, and Kazakhstan's position became known to the world.

I might mention at this point that my only channel of reliable information on events was satellite television. From the morning of August 19 onwards, the television set in my office was permanently switched on and tuned in to CNN, which carried live broadcasts from the streets and squares of Moscow. Thus we were able to follow the rapidly developing course of events.

Anxiety was increasing. On the evening of August 20, Boris Yeltsin managed, almost miraculously, to contact me via the only high-frequency communication line in operation in the building of the Russian Supreme Soviet. He was in a very emotional state. After giving a brief outline of his estimation of the situation, he said that very probably there would be an attempt to seize the building that night, and asked for any assistance we could give. My first thought was to fly out immediately to Moscow, but Yeltsin was categorically opposed to the idea, hinting that the journey might prove dangerous: "Don't take a step outside your republic, Nursultan! In the present situation, your home is your fortress. Take action in Alma-Ata." Accepting this advice, I immediately telephoned Kriuchkov. The chairman of the KGB assured me categorically that no such attack was planned. Realizing that I could not trust his word, I hurriedly rang Yanayev and expressed my rigorous protest, warning him in no uncertain terms that any armed action against the Russian Supreme Soviet would have the most serious consequences. I then rang Yazov and told him that it was criminal to stain one's hands with the blood of the young people defending their President. It would seem that this had its effect, because only a few minutes later one of Yeltsin's assistants informed me that tank movement toward the building had come to a halt.

There were other unpleasant moments when I had to risk all my authority in an effort to prevent, or at least somehow parry the feverish actions of the so-called Emergency Committee. Among these I would include the attempt to bring pressure to bear on our nearest neighbour—the republic of Kirghizia. At 1.30 am on August 21, President Akayev informed me that he had information indicating preparations to bring troops into Bishkek. Urgent intervention was needed to override the very idea of such a punitive measure.

In short, right up to the shameful end of the putsch, up to that joyous moment when Gorbachev telephoned from the Crimea, we were involved in tense and exhausting efforts. It is with a sense of gratitude that I would like to state that during these hours, so fateful for the country and our republic, I never felt alone. Surely, it is at times of need that one discovers one's true friends and allies. I received enormous moral support from the deputies of Kazakhstan, who adopted an unequivocal and uncompromising position vis-a-vis those who had encroached upon our democratic achievements and who, feigning concern for the people, were attempting to force the country back into the chains of a totalitarian regime.

It should be said that the political stability and ethnic harmony which had been achieved in the republic revealed themselves to the full in those difficult days. Both the people and the government of Kazakhstan, and the various public movements, were unanimous in their view of the situation, and united in their efforts. This enabled us to act boldly in defense of democracy without having to look over our shoulder, and to reject totally this counterattack by shameless political bandits.

However, while in no way underestimating the unconditional victory won by the democratic forces, and also the political and moral awareness of the people, which has grown enormously over the years of perestroika, and which became, in effect, the main obstacle facing the conspirators, we cannot ignore the lesson taught us by these tragic events which shook the whole country. With what confidence we used to repeat, only a short while ago, the almost cliched phrase: perestroika is irreversible! Today, it seems to me, we do not have such unshakable confidence. Democratic changes directed only at the political sphere and altering little in the economic base proved to be less stable than we had thought. This was the weak point at which the organizers of the "state of emergency" delivered their main blow.

However worn and threadbare the formulas in the statements issued by the members of the self-appointed "Soviet leadership," they contain a fairly precise diagnosis of the numerous "illnesses" afflicting our society. These include the collapse of the economy and labor discipline the failure to fulfill production norms and contractual obligations, spiralling prices and falling living standards, a ubiquitous mafia and rising crime, and the escalation of armed ethnic conflicts. Such is the list of negative phenomena which indeed provoke widespread discontent among working people. Yet did we not know about all of this before? Of course we did and, moreover, we tried to draw the President's attention to it.

At the 4th Congress of People's Deputies of the USSR I was sharply critical of Gorbachev's sluggishness in political and economic policy, and of inconsistency in the decisions adopted. Neither he nor the government drew the necessary conclusions, and to put it frankly, themselves took the country into a state of emergency. Despite my respect for Gorbachev as the man who launched perestroika, despite my sympathy for all he had to live through during the putsch, I am nonetheless obliged to be harshly critical.

It was at this same fourth congress that Yanayev, one of Gorbachev's closest associates, and one of those who was to betray him, was elected. His name was put forward as a candidate by none other than Gorbachev himself. I remember how, during a break between sessions, when Yanayev had not gained a sufficient number of votes in the first round, I asked the President why he had proposed Yanayev, amazed at his choice. Gorbachev gave no reply, but stubbornly continued to defend his candidate and did not even wish to hear of any alternative.

An extremely negative role was played by the chairman of the Supreme Soviet of the USSR, Lukyanov, who in effect assisted the Emergency Committee, and by the entire Cabinet of Ministers of the USSR was sought to implement the anti-constitutional plans of the Committee. Such was the appointments policy which led to tragedy. Then there are the bloody ethnic conflicts, whose growing intensity was due to the indecisive, extremely vague position adopted by the President on this urgent issue affecting the health and lives of people.

It would be no violation of the truth to say that the President was also responsible for the delay in signing the Union treaty. Apparently under the spell of the central bureaucratic machine and influential representatives of the military-industrial complex, Gorbachev was prejudiced against, and even distrustful of, the republics' legitimate desire to assert their sovereignty and establish horizontal inter-republican links — the basis of the Union treaty. As a result, valuable time was lost, and this played into the hands of Yanahev and his group. They well realized that the Union treaty and the decisive shift to a market economy which it pre-supposed would deliver the final blow to the totalitarian system, and make the huge central apparatus redundant. Accustomed to being in command, this monster was losing its power.

Thus delay by Gorbachev gave the members of the putsch time to draw up a plan of action and strike at the most critical moment, when there was just one day left to the signing of the treaty. They did not waste time. Only recently it has become known that Kriuchkov, former chairman of the KGB, was able to listen in to private talks in Gorbachev's office. I remember that in June or July 1991, when Yeltsin and I met the President of the USSR in his office at Novo-Ogaryovo in order to exchange views on issues pertaining to the "9 + 1" agreement, I was surprised to notice that during the conversation Yeltsin felt unable to speak frankly. When mentioning certain names he would lower his voice, and he avoided controversial topics. Then he even went out onto the balcony to see if anyone was in the vicinity. I asked him jokingly if he thought someone was listening in on us, and he nodded. Gorbachev threw up his hands as if to say: What—in my office?! Later, however, it turned out that the President of Russia was right: our private conversation was recorded in full and given to the future leaders of the putsch.

In short, I believe that Gorbachev must bear his share of responsibility for what happened.

Let us return, however, to the events of August 21. By the afternoon I already had no doubt that the putsch had failed. The government telephones were silent, as if disconnected. I learned that Yanayev, Kriuchkov and Yazov had left Moscow by plane. But where were they going? To be honest, it never occurred to me that they would go to the Crimea and attempt to seek protection from the very President they had removed from power. Moreover, CNN had suggested that the Committee members were flying to Kirghizia or Kazakhstan to seek political asylum. Despite the total absurdity of such a theory, I nonetheless ordered civil aviation chiefs to verify.

Still nothing was known of the fate of Gorbachev, and this particularly worried me. I was convinced that the Committee, faced with the collapse of the putsch, would stop at nothing. Therefore, when the long-awaited telephone call from Foros came, I can honestly say that my joy knew no bounds. I now even find it difficult to reconstruct the sequence of my conversation with Gorbachev, so powerful were the emotions of the moment. I will never forget, however, the unusually intimate tone of his agitated voice, from which it was impossible not to appreciate the enormous shock this man had suffered.

The President thanked me for my support, and asked me to express his gratitude to all the people of Kazakhstan, who had revealed during these difficult days their loyalty to the principles of freedom and democracy and to the lawfully elected state authorities of the USSR. He also informed me that the putschists Baklanov, Yazov, Kriuchkov and Tizyakov were at that moment waiting to see him, and that he had agreed to speak to them only after contacting me and Yeltsin.

Our conversation lasted no more than ten minutes. I put down the receiver and relaxed for the first time during those three days. In my office the television was still showing CNN. People came in and tried to talk to me, but I continued to sit motionless, hearing and seeing nothing. The thought suddenly struck me that no one except myself knew that everything was over. I looked at my watch — 9.30 pm. Kazakh television was showing the official Moscow news programme Vremya. That meant that everyone was now sitting in front of their television sets. It was an excellent opportunity. I left straight away for the television center. Naturally I was not expected there, and when my assistants had found a free studio for me and asked the television crew to interrupt transmission for a special broadcast, the crew began to protest that this was quite impossible. Only when they had confirmed for themselves that the President of Kazakhstan in person was sitting in front of the camera did they agree to put me immediately on the air.

I informed the people of Kazakhstan about my telephone conversation with Gorbachev, that he was in good health and had resumed his duties. I also passed on the words of thanks for the resolute stance adopted by the republic during the days of the coup, and congratulated everyone with the victory. When I left the studio it was suddenly discovered that in the midst of the rush they had forgotten to make a video copy. I had to return to the studio and repeat the message I had just broadcast — and I admit that I did so with the greatest pleasure.

Happy and in high spirits I returned to my office where, despite the late hour, almost all the members of government, and my assistants, had gathered. I have never kept drink in my office, but a bottle of champagne appeared, and on this occasion I did not refuse . . .

That evening we had a great deal to talk about. The putsch had served to open our eyes, and each of us sensed that decisive changes were in the offing which would radically alter our concept of the future Union and of the role of political structures in society. So it proved to be. Today we are facing a very different situation which requires a complete re-assessment not only of strategy and tactic, but of the general concept of state construction. Life itself had taught us a major lesson in genuine democracy, revealing the fragility of the previous construction of the Union treaty, as a result of which it collapsed, and a wholly new model of a community of sovereign states emerged. This community is based not on the customary ideological postulates and political compromises, but on the only possible solid foundation — the unconditional recognition of the freedom and independence of the republics, on mutually beneficial economic cooperation within one common democratic framework.

As a result of the bitter struggle between the forces of reaction and the forces of renewal, the former Union took its farewell, and the republics assumed responsibility for the future of the country. There are those who now see this as a tragedy. Yet is that really so? I was always a passionate supporter of the Novo-Ogaryovo agreements. I never delivered a speech, be it at a plenum or congress or for the mass media, without insisting on the need to sign the Union treaty as quickly as possible. Nor do I now take back those words, although I clearly see the idealism of my former concepts. What has happened was bound to happen. The last argument used by the dying administrative-command system, for whom the signing of the Union treaty was the equivalent of a death sentence, has proved this convincingly. Nor did the putsch extend its life. On the contrary, it only accelerated democratic processes. In the resultant political situation, however, the "9 + 1" formula had become non-viable, and the Novo-Ogaryovo draft treaty had become hopelessly out of date even before it could be implemented.

Today I realize that time was needed to appreciate this new reality, but some were blinded by the euphoria of victory. The endless celebratory demonstrations in Moscow expressing the understandable pride of the victors became increasingly undemocratic in nature. The statements of certain politicians, including some at the very top, began to reveal imperialist, at times even chauvinistic overtones. The public was encouraged to believe in the Messianic role of Russia, which had yet again offered itself in sacrifice to save the peoples of the country from the chains of totalitarianism. This, however, totally ignored the role played by the other republics, and indeed at times one could even hear wholly unfounded accusations that they had supported the Emergency Committee.

It was with growing bewilderment that I listened to such statements broadcast by central television across the whole of the country. Bewilderment gave way to a sense of bitterness when neither Gorbachev nor Yeltsin did anything to counter such an interpretation of events, did not consider it necessary to shed any light on the issue. This is in no way to deny that, in celebrating the victory of democratic forces, we should and must express our deep gratitude to the people of Moscow, to the Russian Supreme Soviet, and to President Yeltsin personally for the decisive and uncompromising position they adopted in this tragic situation. Yet have we any right to forget about all those who opposed the forces of reaction in every region of the country? I could only engage in conjecture: was this simply crude ambition or elementary forgetfulness or was it a deliberate attempt to replace the dictatorship of the fallen center with the dictatorship of the Russian Federation?

It was obvious to any clear-thinking person that the empire had collapsed, and that now we had to climb free of the ruins with as little loss as possible in order to begin the construction of a radically new kind of state. In my opinion we had at the time a good chance of success. Mental inertia, however, can have fateful consequences, and at times one is forced to recognize that even the boldest and most progressive thinkers can fall victim to it. Such was the case on this occasion. At the very moment when unity and joint effort were vitally necessary, there occurred an event which muddied relations between the sovereign republics. I am referring to the memorable ultimatum by Russia to the effect that she reserved the right to make territorial claims against other republics. This statement was provoked by the Ukraine's declaration of independence.

The reaction in the Ukraine and Kazakhstan was immediate and sharp. There followed a series of urgent telephone conversations with Yeltsin, who, to be frank, was not able to offer any comprehensible explanation for this move, and in the end passed it off as an unfortunate statement by his press secretary. We, not unnaturally, were not satisfied by this diversionary tactic over an issue of such vital importance to the republics as that of borders.

This was the tense situation in which the USSR Supreme Soviet began its extraordinary session on August 26. Ironically, this session had been convened by the Emergency Committee in order to legalize its existence. On listening to the speeches made by the deputies, I was increasingly convinced that certain forces were seeking to exploit the political situation exclusively to the benefit of Russia, that is, were seeking to create a federation under the auspices of the Russian Federation with no regard for the sovereignty of the other republics. The Ukraine, Belorussia, Uzbekistan and others also clearly sensed this trend toward the reanimation of an imperialist mentality one might have thought was laid to rest once and for all. It was not impossible to remain silent any longer. At the risk of damaging relations with the Russian leaders, and with Boris Yeltsin, whom I deeply respect, I went to the podium on the second day of the session. What follows is the slightly abridged text of my speech.

". . . An acute feeling of anxiety for the future of the country makes it necessary to reflect on the problems before us and which, as recent days have shown, are far from resolved. All of us today have undergone a major change in our way of thinking, and this obliges us to take a fresh look at the future of the Union and the Union treaty. As you know, I was strongly in favour of signing it as quickly as possible, and I remain so. However, the situation has altered radically, recent events have shown that the old conception of things is potentially explosive, liable to lead to bloody conflicts. We did not heed the words of Andrei Sakharov, who proposed that the Union be a community of equal republics. Now the time has come for us to appreciate the truth of those words. For me it is clear that the renewed Union can no longer be a federation.

"How do I imagine this future Union? First of all, we must conclude contractual economic agreements. Kazakhstan has a wide range of economic relations with all those who agree to such cooperation. To go our separate ways now would bring no economic benefit to any of the 15 republics. Moreover, certain functions remain with the central organs. In my opinion, these functions should consist of the defense of our common borders, control over nuclear arms, foreign policy, a single system of transport and communications, etc.

". . . We are used to the abbreviation USSR. I think it should become the FUSR—the Free Union of Sovereign Republics [in Russian, the acronym would remain the same—Tr.]. By republics I mean all the republics, including the autonomous republics which have declared or wish to declare their sovereignty. In short, I propose the conclusion of a confederated agreement. I am convinced that only then will we be able to achieve true equality. The conclusion of a non economic agreement can take place only in a calm and stable situation, and only with those republics who fully guarantee human rights and trust each other. We must ensure the protection of human rights for everyone, regardless of nationality, creed or party (except, of course, fascist) on our territory in accord with the Helsinki Agreement. To this end Kazakhstan is prepared to be the first to invite an international commission to operate on a permanent basis in our multinational republic. We wish to put a complete end to the violations of human rights which we have inherited from the old system. We are also prepared to invite an international commission of experts to examine those who are in mental hospitals. We are beginning immediately the review of all so-called economic crimes, the majority of which were merely ordinary business activity. We consider all this to be the precondition of building a law-governed state, and the guarantee of republican sovereignty.

"I propose that we settle immediately the question of recognizing the independence of the Baltic republics, Moldova, Georgia and all those who have expressed their desire to achieve independence in a lawful, democratic manner. Moreover, this must be done without any presentation of bills for billions of rubles, since even one human life is beyond price.

". . . The new Union should not have any Union cabinet of ministers, no Union parliament, nothing except the agreed relations the republics have entered into. Today we face the moment of truth, and I cannot imagine any other basis on which Kazakhstan will enter a union with other republics. So much for strategy, so to speak. As for tactic, over the immediate future, this should consist in the rapid formation of a transitional inter-republican economic council with equal representation of all those republics who have united in an economic community. Prior to this, we must make it possible for all those who have decided to leave the Union to do so, but maintain economic cooperation with them. For I realize that, while leaving politically, they will continue to cooperate with the remaining republics economically. Such, in outline, is my view of the future Union.

"In conclusion I would like to emphasize that no one should have any illusions. Kazakhstan will never consent to be the 'appendage' of another region, and will never be anyone's 'little brother'. We will enter the Union with equal rights and equal opportunities."

The main idea expressed in my speech was supported by all the republics. On that same day, August 27, I attended a meeting of the President of the USSR, Gorbachev, the President of the Russian Federation, Yeltsin, and the President of the Republic of Kirghizia, Akayev. We reiterated our support for the Novo-Ogaryovo process, and expressed our hopes for the rapid conclusion of a Union treaty. Its necessary amendments dictated by the new situation in the country, would contribute to political stability and open up new opportunities for the implementation of reforms, the creation of a single market, and the conclusion of an economic agreement among all the sovereign states. In the course of our conversation serious doubts were expressed as to the expediency of creating separate national armies, excluding the possible formation of small units of a national guard. The main reason for this view was appreciated of the fact that the Soviet Union is a nuclear power.

I was particularly gratified to hear Yeltsin state his position, this time clearly and unambiguously, as regards territorial issues. He said that, as far as Russia was concerned, such questions could only arise if a state bordering on the Russian Federation left the USSR.

Yeltsin repeated this argument when the two of us met together that same day. We again confirmed our recognition of the declarations of sovereignty made by the republics of the USSR, and also of the treaties and agreements concluded by them. We were also of the same opinion regarding the need to preserve the unity of the Union armed forces. Apparently aware of my concern over the border issue, the President of

Russia stressed yet again at the end of our meeting that, in relations with Union states, Russia would abide by the principle of the inviolability of existing boundaries.

Only two days later a delegation headed by Alexander Rutskoi, Vice-President of Russia, flew out to Kiev and then, immediately afterwards, to Alma-Ata. Rutskoi, an ex-colonel of the air force who fought in Afghanistan, and was promoted to the rank of major-general for his resolute action during the putsch, analyzed the complex situation with characteristic realism. The talks were concluded within one day. In a joint communique we confirmed all the clauses of the Treaty and of the bilateral agreements concluded between Kazakhstan and Russia two weeks previously in Alma-Ata. To our mutual satisfaction we both noted that the border issue had been definitively relegated to the past.

In the late evening of August 31, I received unexpected support for my new position on the future Union. The former prime minister of Great Britain, Margaret Thatcher, made a brief stopover at Alma-Ata airport on her way from London to Tokyo. In fact this stopover had initially been planned for Tashkent, but Mrs Thatcher had changed her plans while still in flight, and had chosen to have a meeting with me. I have always considered it a great honor to talk with this intelligent, and exceptionally charming woman — an international politician of the first order. On this occasion also my expectations were justified. I was very happy to learn that government and business circles in Great Britain were very interested in my position regarding the future organization of the country and republican sovereignty, and that they supported the economic initiatives taking place in Kazakhstan. We parted on cordial terms. The sound advice and good wishes expressed by Mrs Thatcher further strengthened my belief that the political line I had been supporting over recent years was the right one.

Modification of the political and economic policy after the putsch was, however, inevitable. This was the view of the republican leaders and the President of the USSR on the eve of the extraordinary Congress of People's Deputies of the USSR, which began on September 2, 1991. Our joint Statement, drawn up literally just a few hours before the opening of the congress, introduced a major change into the agenda and had an explosive effect. I frankly admit that, when I went to the podium with the text I had been given to read, I was extremely nervous, for I realized that many of the deputies would not agree with our proposals. At the same time, I was firmly convinced that only a radical change of course could bring us out of the political impasse, that only the republics were now able to assume the powers of the defunct center, and responsibility for the future of the peoples of the country.

The debates were heated. Happily common sense prevailed. The congress adopted a number of fundamental documents opening up the way for accelerated reform, guaranteeing republican declarations of sovereignty and giving them concrete content. I am thinking in particular of the law "On the organs of state power and administration of the USSR in the transitional period," and "The declaration of individual rights and freedoms." Thus we now have a bicameral Supreme Soviet. One chamber — the Council of Republics — is composed of People's Deputies of the USSR elected by the republican parliaments, while the second — the Union Council — is composed of republican deputations seconded by their respective parliaments. A State Council and an Inter-Republican Economic Committee have been formed to coordinate and supervise the economy. It should be stressed that during the transitional period the Constitution of the USSR will function only insofar as it does not contradict the above-mentioned Law.

What does all of this mean? One can state unequivocally that we now live in a qualitatively different country, that the imperial card has been trumped once and for all. Now what matters is to maintain stability so that we can arrive at the signing of the Union treaty (and I am convinced that it will be signed) in a civilized manner. We must unite on qualitatively new principles which take into account the wishes of the republics, who will themselves determine the form of their participation in the Union. Some will join as members of a federation, some on a confederal basis. Associated membership is also possible. This pluralism of relations is the most important prerequisite of a genuine community free from any kind of political pressure or ideological fetishism.

I cannot but express regret that the decisions adopted at the extraordinary Congress of People's Deputies of the USSR were, of course, belated. If something similar had been done a couple of years earlier, we would have been able to create a Union of genuinely equal republics, retain the membership of all the subjects of the Union, avoid ethnic conflicts and, of course, progress much further with our reforms. Such is the price of delay, of the inability or unwillingness to make a sober assessment of reality. Nor can I omit to mention in this connection the very compromising role played by the conservative section of the party apparatus.

Could it have been otherwise? In all probability, no. In effect the Communist Party had lost control over the party administrative machine, which had developed over the decades as a parasite on the party and had become an unconstitutional but all-powerful state system. It had penetrated into the whole of society from top to bottom, paralyzing the mass of party members, depriving them of any initiative, manipulating their opinion as it wished. The April breeze had not entered the corridors of party power. It is not surprising, therefore, if today the democratic storm now blasts through these corridors, sweeping away that which has become outdated.

The explosion came during the coup d'etat. Certain members of the top leadership of the party proved to have been involved, and this finally destroyed what little authority the party, and in particular its administrative organs, still retained. In these circumstances I felt obliged to make a very difficult and painful decision. On August 22 I publicly announced my resignation from the Politburo and Central Committee of the CPSU, and then also from the post of first secretary of the Central Committee of the Communist Party of Kazakhstan. There were, it is true, those who warned me that this step would alienate rank-and-file party members, and that I would lose their support. I replied that for me it was a question of conscience and honor, that I was compelling no one to follow my example, but acting as I believed necessary. I can now say that the support of the thousands of communists and non-party people who sent me letters and telegrams expressing their agreement with my decision convinced me that I had acted rightly.

I am also convinced that I acted rightly when, at an extraordinary plenum of the party, I proposed that the Communist Party of Kazakhstan leave the CPSU, and that the republican Central Committee cease its activity. The Central Committee of the CPSU had ceased to exist as a unified structure, and there could be no return. Any attempted cosmetic reform of the party was doomed to failure. However difficult it might be, it was necessary to reject the communist dogma which had been inculcated into us for decades. Communist ideology is incompatible in principle with such concepts as capital, the market, and particularly private property. While proclaiming freedom of speech, conscience and the press, the party apparatus had instituted total censorship and eradicated in embryo any initiative or democracy both within the party and outside it. Concealing itself behind a fig leaf of the attractive slogans of communism, the party bureaucracy had shamelessly exploited the people, played on their genuine enthusiasm for work, their noblest patriotic and international sentiments, their desire for a better freer life, for equality and social justice. Built on false postulates, this ideology objectively could not win the historical argument with the other system of social development, which had convincingly demonstrated its viability across the rest of the globe. We cannot but recognize that this ideology is totally discredited. Is there any point, therefore, when thinking of the future, in clinging to outworn dogma? That would be, to say the least, unnatural.

The other lesson is that there is little point in democratic changes directed only at the political sphere and having almost no effect on the economic base. While giving my whole-hearted support to democracy, freedom of speech and pluralism of opinion, I cannot accept disagreement and discord in the economic sphere, which at the present moment requires above all precision and clarity. The crisis can be overcome, and the shift to a market economy made only if there is a rigorous prohibition on any party, political or ideological interference in these processes.

I would like to state in this connection that our desire for economic sovereignty is in no way a denial of the principles of integration and a single market. These in their turn require efficient inter-republican structures. At present we are coming up against a certain degree of resistance on the part of some republics, who, for certain political and other reasons, are dragging their feet over the signing of an economic community agreement. This was illustrated, for example, at the meeting of the leaders of thirteen sovereign republics at Alma-Ata. While I believe this meeting to have been highly successful, there is nonetheless one main factor still delaying economic cooperation, namely the absence of any genuine market links among the republics. In these circumstances, any economic dependence is feared, and becomes not a consolidating factor, as elsewhere in the world, but a divisive one.

With time this situation must inevitably change, and we will together move toward the idea of a common market, without which it will prove impossible to integrate into contemporary civilization. I will go further. Objective economic expedience will oblige us to create a common market that is open, and that presupposes the broad and diverse participation of Western enterprise.

The events of August shook not only the USSR but the whole world. The specter of totalitarianism assumed tangible reality, a nightmarish fact in the face of which all democratic forces united. Their victory, however, did not become the beginning of consolidation among the republics. On the contrary, we witnessed the acceleration of centrifugal processes. What, in your opinion, is the explanation?

Indeed, at first glance it might seem that all the obstacles along the path to the Union treaty have been eliminated. However, the roots of the imperialist tradition which has weighed down on us for several centuries, up to and including the twentieth, proved too deep. Even now, in a radically new situation, they can, unfortunately, still be detected within victorious democracy. Both in the Ukraine and in Kasakhstan it required no little effort to overcome friction in our relations with Russia, and to prevent within a matter of hours the unpredictable consequences of the notorious statement on possible territorial claims. Although the status quo was restored, the ripples had spread wide. Under pressure from a concerned public, the republics were obliged to issue firm statements on their freedom and independence, on their unwillingness to continue in the humiliating role of "little brothers".

It is no secret that in the euphoria of victory there were those who attempted to accuse the republics of having failed to display the necessary decisiveness in their estimation of events. What can we say on this subject? Kazakhstan does not accept such accusation. Our position during those dark days was unambiguous—support for democracy and legality. However, that is only one aspect of the question. The other, perhaps more important aspect is that any accusations of this kind divide the republics into "innocent" and "guilty", and operate against our newly-emerging political and economic community. In the final analysis it must be honestly recognized that the victory over the totalitarian system was secured not only by Muscovites and the Russian parliament led by Yeltsin, but by all the peoples of the country without exception. In the squares of Alma-Ata and Tbilisi, Baku and Kishinev, Vilnius and Yerevan blood was shed and lives sacrificed for the victory of democracy.

There is yet another threat manifesting itself today. I am referring to the fact that on the wave of a democratic upsurge there may appear the foam of chauvinism, and this will inevitably lead to counter-action in the republics and generate a further spiral in ethnic conflicts. This must not be allowed to happen under any circumstances.

Our past experience of life in a totalitarian state, the basic fear of finding oneself yet again in a subordinate position, impedes political integration. It is no coincidence that the word "Union" provokes a storm of negative reaction in the republics. This means that time is needed for things to settle down. I myself believe it to be inevitable that our future political coalition will take the form of a confederation — a union of sovereign states. Within the competence of this Union will come such important issues of state as the declaration of war and conclusion of peace, the conclusion of alliances and agreements with foreign states by the subjects of the confederation on a common basis, questions of defence, railway, air and maritime transport, atomic power, the banking, post and communications network, etc. I would like to emphasize that the very nature of the coalition already indicates that it will be a fundamentally different kind of political association, wholly different from the former USSR. In my opinion, both the Union and autonomous republics of the former USSR should become equal subjects of the confederation.

I am convinced that sooner or later we will certainly arrive at a political union. Even now we are acutely aware of the lack of an effective mechanism for regulating relations among the sovereign republics and their political institutions at every level. I never weary of repeating that we should look at Western Europe, at the member countries of the Common Market. None of them lacks sovereignty, yet integration obliges them to seek ways of creating an inter-state community. Guided by economic expediency and common sense, these countries have created a whole range of joint political structures, and harmonizing specific elements in their foreign policy has become standard practice. Consequently we should not simply dismantle everything, only to have to traverse the same path yet again, expending effort and time to invent that which has long since been invented. Decentralization should not be taken to an absurd extreme.

I was also convinced that the economy cannot be revitalized unless we proceed immediately to signing an economic agreement among the republics. In my view this should be a wholly non-political document whose purpose is to recreate a unified economic territory and establish stable relations among the republics. The agreement which has now been signed specifies quite clearly those questions of socio-economic policy which come within the competence of Union organs. Together we are drawing up the principles of a single monetary and credit policy, Union and republican budgets, including the objects and scale of Union expenditure, a common price policy, a common foreign policy, and a number of others.

If we turn to the question of membership of the Union, then the principles of trade and economic relations with republics which have not signed the economic agreement should be set out in a special section. We have contracts and agreements with Russia, the Ukraine, Belorussia, Estonia, Uzbekistan, Kirghizia, Tadzhikistan, Turkmenia and Azerbaijan, and these may have a considerable influence on our fulfillment of obligations, and on the assertion of our independence in the settlement of regional problems. The Alma-Ata meeting of the leaders of thirteen sovereign republics was of particular importance in strengthening economic ties. I can say without fear of exaggeration that it is of tremendous potential significance. We were able to achieve major progress toward agreement on the question of an economic community treaty as the basis of long-term constructive cooperation. It is gratifying to note that, at this difficult period in the country's history, it is Kazakhstan which is acting as a major positive factor in internal affairs, as a generator of initiatives aimed at preserving a unified economic territory and promoting social stability. This is to the credit of our republic, adds to its prestige, and is the direct consequence of all that has been done to create the basis for Kazakhstan's state sovereignty and national independence.

The results of this meeting exceeded even our most optimistic expectations. Eight republics signed the document on a single economic territory. It was, of course, no easy task to secure this victory for common sense. Indeed, there was one moment of apparent impasse when I was obliged to declare that, even if only three republics remain together, we would nonetheless sign the agreement and not permit final disintegration. This firm position made it possible to halt the fatal process of division, to take the first step toward a qualitatively new association of republics, and to inject real meaning into their declarations of sovereignty.

Taken overall, the Alma-Ata meeting was seen by all as a good portent, as a sign of hope that we would preserve that community of nations which is linked together by a common history. It is within our power to ensure that this hope is realized.

You have said more than once that the Communist Party of Kazakhstan is quite strong, that the communists of the republic, unlike those of the central party apparatus, support the political reforms that are underway, and are actively cooperating in the introduction of market relations. Nonetheless, the implacable logic of events led the republican party organization to declare itself dissolved. Do you not think that your previous assessment of the role of the Communist Party was mistaken?

As an integral part of the CPSU, the Communist Party of Kazakhstan could not avoid distortions, and our party structures proved not to be equal to the situation. Many of them were hopelessly behind the times, and had lost touch with the mass of the party membership, not to say the mass of the people as a whole. However radical the laws we passed, however promising the programs to overcome the crisis and move to a market economy—whatever measures were taken, party leaders and party committees would, at best, remain passive, and on occasion offer silent resistance, blocking constructive change. Such a situation could not continue.

I would like to emphasize yet again that this in no way relates to primary party organizations, and in particular work collectives and rank-and-file communists and party veterans. They understood and accepted the process of renewal and supported the process of democratization which began in the republic, the shift toward new economic relations and to progressive forms and methods of management.

The facts of the situation, however, cannot be ignored. If we had continued in our attempts somehow to preserve the old party structures, we would undoubtedly have lost the support of the millions of ordinary communists and workers of Kazakhstan. Moreover, I myself can see quite clearly that we need a radically new party which will see its goal not as the achievement of the scholastic ideals of a so-called bright future, only dimly understood by the people, but the achievement of concrete humanistic objectives, and above all the social protection of citizens, their rights and freedoms, and ethnic harmony. It must certainly be a parliamentary-style party which has wholly rejected the old principles of organization and work among the people. It will fight for its place in the political structure of society by lawful, constitutional means, and use its influence only for the benefit of the working people. And, of course, it will carry on a constructive dialogue, based on equality and mutual respect, with all democratic parties and movements.

During the days of the putsch we became painfully aware that the people are hostage to Union structures over which they have no control, such as the KGB, the Ministry of Defense, the Ministry of Internal Affairs, and the military-industrial complex. What steps is Kazakhstan taking to exclude in the future the possibility of using these structures for anti-constitutional purposes, and also to create an effective system of collective security?

Republican participation in military affairs is one of the essential aspects involved in sovereignty. While not rejecting the idea of maintaining united armed forces and border troops, we intend to ensure that our relations with the armed forces stationed in Kazakhstan are on a rigorously legal basis, and that the President of Kazakhstan shares equal command over them. With this in view I have issued a decree on the creation of a Committee of Defense in the republic and on subjecting the KGB and the

Ministry of Internal Affairs to the exclusive jurisdiction of the republican authorities.

A major factor in strengthening the security of the republic is the creation of a national guard. This is a perfectly legitimate and necessary step, if one recalls the tragic events of August.

In accord with another decree, recruitment into the armed forces, beginning in the autumn of 1991, will come under the direct control of the republican state authorities. First we will bring up to strength the units on our own territory, and only then will a small contingent of our recruits be sent outside Kazakhstan to serve with the navy, the air force and as paratroopers.

We are being actively supported by public organizations and movements in our efforts to ensure that the military cease to have a free hand and do as they like on the territory of Kazakhstan. The closure of the Semipalatinsk nuclear testing ground is proof of this. I hope that our government will soon begin talks on the future of other military testing grounds located in our republic.

As for nuclear weapons, I am well aware that my position on this issue is of considerable interest to the world at large. I wish to state firmly and clearly that Kazakhstan will never become hostage to the nuclear arsenal on its territory. We shall take all the necessary measures to ensure reliable double control over the strategic missiles located on our territory. I am convinced that this control should be exercised within the framework of a unified defense system, and with the participation of representatives of Kazakhstan. In addition we shall do all we can to promote a radical reduction in strategic offensive arms in accord with the Soviet-American agreement.

One of the most important elements in state stability is that of ethnic relations, and this element becomes many times more significant with transition to a market economy. How do you assess the prospects for resolving the ethnic conflicts that have already flared up? What is the position of multi-ethnic Kazakhstan on this issue?

As was pointed out at the recent Moscow Conference on the Human Dimension, an important factor in promoting the development of economic cooperation is to resolve the problem of human rights in the USSR. In particular, foreign politicians and businessmen are seriously concerned over the ethnic conflicts which continue to disrupt various regions of the country. Above all, however, it is our grief and our tragedy. Now that the centre has collapsed and has revealed its total inability to exert any influence on the course of events, Russia and Kazakhstan have taken on the difficult task of seeking to resolve the Armenian-Azerbaijan conflict. I am sure that the authority enjoyed by our sovereign republics will help to end the bloodshed and bring peace to these suffering people. True, it is an extremely difficult task requiring the maximum of physical and moral effort.

When I went to Nagorno-Karabakh together with Boris Yeltsin I saw once again with my own eyes how fragile and vulnerable relations between ethnic groups can prove to be, and what enormous grief can be inflicted on people by embittered confrontation. In defending the cause of peace in Karabakh, I was defending the cause of peace in our republic, because no borders, no sovereignty, can serve to put out the blaze of ethnic conflict. It can be halted only by the good will of the people, their sense of their enormous responsibility in maintaining truly fraternal, neighborly relations. I hope that the people of Kazakhstan appreciate this fact, and will not permit even the slightest dissonance in our multi-ethnic harmony, not even the hint of ethnic conflict. For its part, the Government of Kazakhstan, and I as President, will continue to pursue a carefully considered nationalities policy and to act promptly to end any provocative actions aimed at undermining our multi-national unity.

I sent a telegram to the Presidium of the Conference on the Human Dimension in which I stated that Kazakhstan, having become a sovereign republic, sees itself as inheriting the obligations assumed by the USSR to the world community on this question, and guarantees human rights to all, regardless of race, creed or party. Furthermore, I expressed my willingness to welcome to Kazakhstan at any time an international commission to verify observance of human rights. I think that this was absolutely the right step to take, and one that brings us closer to the level of truly civilized states.

In Kazakhstan, as in many other republics, the idea of national revival on the basis of state sovereignty has taken hold of the popular mind, and pushed into second place both class and party interests. It is only natural that this should happen. It reflects the collapse of our union within a unitary state, the liberation of nations from the chains of totalitarianism, their long-cherished desire to live not according to instructions, but independently, in freedom. These circumstances have also offered the young Kazakh nation the opportunity to avail itself of the achievements of modern civilization and, guided by the principles of economic expediency and common sense, to make the transition from totalitarianism and economic collapse to democracy and prosperity over a historically brief period of time. When saying this, however, I would like to stress that I am not a supporter of the now "fashionable" assertion that radical economic and democratic reforms are more effective in an ethnically homogeneous state. The specific feature of multi-ethnic Kazakhstan gives it an enormous advantage. Friendship among peoples is not only our main and, perhaps, most unique possession, but also our faith, our hope and our support.

I very much hope that the sovereignty we have achieved during the hard struggles of perestroika will become the guarantee of social progress in my republic, since only free people in a free state can hope for the realization of their most treasured aspirations. I believe that, despite all the difficulties and problems, Kazakhstan will emerge successfully to take a worthy place in the civilized world community.

Nursultan Nazarbaev is the only leader in the former USSR who was able to maintain stability in his republic, and avoid ethnic conflicts. As the first President of Kazakhstan, his political priorities are the introduction of a market economy and the construction of a democratic, law-governed state. His character enables him to combine a calm, thoughtful approach with determination and will power. He is the first president in the world to have stopped nuclear testing on his territory. The resolution displayed by Nazarbaev during the August putsch was a major factor in the victory of democracy.